STRATEGY FOR YOUTH LEADERS

This book is dedicated to Christian youth leaders and youth workers.

May the God of peace, who through the blood of the eternal covenant brought back from the dead our Lord Jesus, that great Shepherd of the sheep, equip you with everything good for doing his will, and may he work in us what is pleasing to him, through Jesus Christ, to whom be glory for ever and ever. Amen (Hebrews 13:20–21).

STRATEGY FOR YOUTH LEADERS

SETTING GOALS, SEEING RESULTS

ROSS FARLEY

Scripture
Union

STRATEGY FOR YOUTH LEADERS
© 1991 Ross Farley

Unless otherwise indicated, all Scripture quotations in this
publication are from the Holy Bible, New International
Version. Copyright © 1973, 1978, 1984 International Bible
Society.

Scripture Union books are published by
ANZEA PUBLISHERS
3-5 Richmond Road
Homebush West NSW 2140

ISBN 0-85892-476-5 (Australia)
      0-86201-763-7 (United Kingdom)

Cover design by David Wong
Cover photograph by Graeme Horner
Diagrams by Alex Grancha (Green Hornet Graphics)
Typeset by Adtype Graphics Pty Ltd, North Sydney, NSW
Printed in Singapore by Singapore National Printers

contents

acknowledgments

Apart from scripture quotations, this book contains only one quotation from another writer. That is because this book is largely the product of my own thoughts on youth ministry which have been influenced by people I have met, books and other material I have read as well as many years of experience. The source of most of the material in this book is difficult to pinpoint, but I can identify the following.

Anyone who has read Lawrence Richards will recognise that he has influenced my thinking. Richards' influence is evident not so much in specific points but in general principles that are interwoven throughout this book. I am also conscious that Jay Kesler influenced some ideas that find expression in this book, and that I first came across some ideas in chapter four when using the training manuals of Youth for Christ.

I would like to thank Rick Green who helped with some contacting ideas and everyone who provided information for the stories that are used as illustrations. Finally, I would like to thank all the many youth workers who have worked with me over the years and the students in recent years who have helped to refine my thinking.

introduction

It is my hope and prayer that this book will make a useful contribution to the current literature on youth ministry. Most books on youth ministry are resource books providing ideas for activities, Bible studies, dramas, discussions etc. This book is different in that it attempts to provide a framework in which to use those ideas and resources. Instead of building a youth program based on the ideas that happen to turn up, youth leaders are encouraged to think about their goals and direction and to select carefully the ideas and resources that are likely to achieve these goals. While I welcome the great number of resource books that are on the market, I am convinced that most of the problems in youth groups are more to do with poor modelling and inadequate goals and strategies than with limited resources.

The principles outlined in this book have been successfully implemented in a variety of contexts over a number of years. They have worked effectively in Christian youth groups in church, para-church and school settings, in large as well as small groups and in groups led by full-time youth workers as well as those led by volunteers. However most of the book is written to apply to voluntary youth leaders in a church context because it is expected that these are the people who are most likely to read this book.

Chapter 1 identifies the goal of youth ministry, chapter 2 outlines a strategy and the rest of this book deals with the 'how' of youth ministry. Chapter 3 discusses some 'nuts and bolts' issues which arise when implementing the strategy, and chapters 4 to 6 deal with each step in the strategy.

It seems to be the practice in some youth work to copy aspects of the current youth culture and try to find ways to include the Christian dimension. That is not my approach.

This is not to say that I do not take youth culture seriously; youth ministry *must* be relevant to youth culture. My starting point, however, is not youth culture but effective ministry practice. I take the principles of effective Christian ministry and apply those principles to working with young people in their own culture. Therefore, even though this book has aspects which will date, it is based on principles that are more enduring than the changing whims of western youth culture.

What do we mean by 'young people'? Who are the people this book refers to? I am reluctant to give ages: 'youth' has more to do with the developmental stages of adolescence and young adulthood than any particular age range. It certainly includes teenagers, although adolescence begins for many before the age of thirteen. Many of the dynamics described in this book will begin to lose their force when young people, or their peers, seriously begin to seek a marriage partner. The strategies described in this book will probably work best when young people are in their mid-teens, although most of the basic principles are applicable to people of all ages.

This book does not attempt to address the particular needs of young people who are marginalised, specially troubled or regarded for some reason or other as 'problem' young people. To attempt to deal with such issues in a book of this size and purpose would inevitably lead to a superficial treatment of complex issues. There are all sorts of reasons why some young people are troubled. Some are disadvantaged; some seem to have everything they need and yet are anti-social; some are both disadvantaged and anti-social. Some express their difficulties with aggression, while others quietly withdraw and are less likely to be regarded as 'problems'. To help such people often involves a complex interplay of approaches that may be psychological, social, cultural, medical, educational, economic and spiritual.

The principles outlined in this book can be used to reach out specifically to groups of these 'problem' young people. On the other hand, youth leaders who effectively employ these strategies are likely to find themselves ministering to both 'well-adjusted' and 'problem' young people. When you cast a net into the sea you often catch all kinds of fish.

I have made some comments in this book on the content of the Christian message that we teach. I have kept these to a minimum in order to concentrate more on issues to do with goals, strategies, planning and management. I could write a lot more about the means of communicating the Christian message and the shape of that message—but if I start, where do I stop? Perhaps another time, in another book!

Finally, it needs to be noted that the kind of youth ministry described here cannot usually be put in place overnight. This book will give readers an idea of what to head for, but it may take six months or even two or three years to get all of this happening.

Ross Farley.

▶ ▶

1

where are you headed?

GOALS FOR YOUTH MINISTRY

▶ ▶

John and Lorraine walked into my office, took a seat and began to tell me their troubles. They were the youth leaders of a suburban church and they were experiencing a number of problems. On top of discipline problems, and criticism from church members who all seemed to have different expectations, they were having trouble coming up with ideas for each week's program.

After listening for some time I asked: 'What is the goal you are working towards with this youth group?'

John and Lorraine were both speechless: they really did not know what they were trying to achieve. At first they also had trouble understanding what the question of goals had to do with the issues they were raising. But the lack of clear goals invites criticism and misbehaviour; while a clear idea of what we are trying to achieve helps us to know how to deal with problems and how to choose the appropriate resources for the task.

Our first problem is inside our heads

There are hundreds of people like John and Lorraine: highly involved in youth ministry and yet rarely stopping to think about what it is all supposed to achieve. They are very conscious of the problems they face: problems with youth, parents, church hierarchy and the lack of ideas and resources. But most of them are slow to realise that the first problem we youth workers have to deal with is inside our heads. We look for gimmicks, games and ideas but problems persist because we have not really thought through what we are trying to do. Of course, clear goals do not mean problem free youth work but they do help us to deal with problems and maintain a sense of direction.

INADEQUATE GOALS

Before we consider a biblical goal for youth ministry let us consider three inadequate goals that are commonly held by youth leaders—often unconsciously.

1. The babysitting syndrome

Here the youth leader is seen as a babysitter and *the goal of the youth work is to hold young people in the fellowship.* This is one of the most common goals encountered in youth ministry and it can take a number of forms as follows:

- To hold young people in our youth group so they don't leave the church or join another church or join another group in our church.
- To hold young people in our group so they don't go places

or do things we don't approve of—to keep them enter-
tained under our control. (This is not to suggest that we
should never provide an alternative to specific events that
may occur from time to time—but that is inadequate as a
long-term goal.)

* To hold young people in our fellowship until they outgrow
  the unsettled stage of youth so we can then give them
  responsible tasks and teach them the Christian faith.

What are the problems with this goal?

The youth leader whose goal is to hold young people
usually ends up catering for those who are most likely to
leave at the expense of committed young people. Four issues
will create problems.

(a) The gospel will cause offence. The gospel must be
either accepted or rejected: there is no neutral ground.
Young people who reject the gospel will probably leave
simply because the gospel is being declared. We should
encourage such people to stay in the group but we should
not be surprised if they leave.

Care should be taken when modifying the program to suit
such people. We should examine ourselves when people leave
and look for faults in ourselves and our programs. But if we
water down our programs to hold people who have already
decided to reject Christ, they will probably leave anyhow and
we will have done little to build the lives of the others in the
group. The goal of holding usually leads us to back off from
the radical demands of the gospel.

Jesus did not try to hold people. There were many, like the
rich young ruler, who found out about Jesus and went away.
Jesus simply let them go. Evangelism polarises people. If we
declare Christ, people will leave because of Christ.

This does not mean that we should not organise events to
attract young people. There is all the difference in the world

between contacting and holding. It is good to do things to attract young people who have not been exposed to the gospel. But that is totally different to changing a program to hold those who no longer wish to hear the gospel or identify with a Christian group.

(b) The image you project. When you water down your program to hold people, you project an image of Christianity that is attractive to no-one. For the young person who wants a night club, the youth group will never do no matter how much it is modified. In the meantime the seeking non-Christians and the committed Christians are also left unsatisfied. The goal of holding drives your program into no-man's land. Few will be committed to that which requires little commitment.

(c) Pressure from people. Part of a youth program I once led was a Bible study that attracted about 80 young people. I well remember one father demanding that we abolish the Bible study simply because his daughters would not come. If our goal is to hold people, it is difficult to deal with that sort of pressure. We won't please everyone no matter what we do. We need a goal that goes beyond mere attendance or we will be tossed around by every bit of pressure.

(d) The maturing processes of young people. As young people mature they will outgrow the youth group. Hopefully they will move on to another context of Christian fellowship that will support and nourish them—maybe an older youth group or the adult fellowship. If the youth leaders have a goal of holding young people in their own group, they can hinder this maturing process.

Youth groups that hold young people

While I have said that the goal of youth ministry should not be to hold young people, it should be recognised that well run youth programs will be attractive to young people and will therefore usually tend to hold them. They will usually be less inclined to do things like leave the church or go to night clubs. In other words effective youth groups will usually hold young people but that should not be the goal. On the other hand youth leaders who make it their aim to hold young people are rarely effective and are least likely to develop the kind of ministry that does hold them.

2. The program syndrome

This goal is simply to run a program for young people. There is not much thought about how the program will help or develop the young people who come: the focus is on the activity itself. Some people enjoy organising programs and as long as people come and it all runs smoothly, that's all that matters. In other instances this goal stems from expectations. Churches compare youth programs and it is embarrassing not to have one. So they start the youth group or keep it going simply for the sake of having it.

A group from one church came and saw me because they were having trouble starting a youth group. When we investigated the district we found that virtually no teenagers lived there; the district was dominated by old people and young adults. I was pleased when they abandoned their plan for a youth group and began a ministry for young adults. In the conversations that took place it became clear that the reason they initially wanted a youth group was that every church was supposed to have one and they felt like the odd church in their denomination. It is very easy to so focus on programs that we lose sight of the people they are supposed to benefit.

Our goals may also focus on some specific aspect of the program. Some people focus on attendance so that the whole purpose is to get more and more young people coming.

Others focus on the quality of the program—ever striving for a smoother presentation. These may be good secondary goals, but if that is what we are primarily concerned with, we can end up with well attended, smoothly run programs that do very little to build up the young people who come.

3. The method syndrome

Just as the running of a program can become an end in itself, so can the maintenance of a method. The real goal of some people is *to maintain a particular method of youth work*. The youth leader's commitment to a particular method can easily override the spiritual and emotional welfare of the young people in the district. It can be any method—a youth rally or club, a coffee-shop, a camping program—but the telltale sign is a refusal to change methods even when the old ones are clearly not working and more effective ones are readily available. The goal has become, not ministry to young people, but the promotion or protection of a particular method.

This situation is repeated time and again. Somebody starts a particular youth program that is effective for some years. But eventually it begins to struggle: there is a steady decline in attendance and leaders become hard to find. The church is harangued about lack of support and the organisers lobby hard with the church leaders to have the program propped up. In spite of everything the decline continues but the organisers refuse to accept that their method is no longer relevant. They will always rationalise their failure and simply refuse to see that the young people have voted with their feet. In order to protect their method they may even oppose anyone who tries to start another youth ministry based on a different method. Of course they want to see young people come to Christ and follow him, but they would like it to happen through their method.

The danger is greatest when ...
The more a method is institutionalised, the greater this danger becomes. The more the particular method has committees, manuals, membership, uniforms, awards and flags, the greater the likelihood that the method will become the goal. It becomes entrenched, with more people having a vested interest in keeping the method in operation.

The more useful a method has been in the past the greater is the danger of the method becoming the goal, because leaders may attempt to reproduce the past rather than minister to the present. People often develop an emotional attachment to the types of programs in which they came to Christ and grew in their youth. When they become leaders they want today's young people to experience their yesterday so they hang on to methods that have outlived their usefulness.

Locked in on one method
When the method becomes the goal you get locked in to one particular approach. Then, as times change and young people change, you are unable to adjust adequately and you become trapped in ineffective methods. Of course, limited changes are allowed but the basic program model must be maintained whether it is effective or not. We must keep that coffee-shop or boys' club going!

Spanners are used for one task and hammers for another. So in youth ministry we should be able to use the method that is most appropriate to the task at hand and then put it away. But the task is not to run camps, coffee-shops or boys' clubs; the task is the development of young people. The methods are really the tools we use to help achieve that task.

We need wisdom to know which methods are the most suitable for our task and when to replace a particular method. No one method will be suitable for all young people all of the time. Methods that help some may not help others; a method that is useful in one era may not be so useful in another; methods that reach one age-group may leave another group cold.

Some youth leaders are reluctant to change methods because they see it as an admission of failure. But the successful youth leader recognises when changing conditions demand a change of method. Those who refuse to examine the alternatives are heading for failure in the long run. It is safest to assume that the best methods for ministering to today's young people have not yet been discovered.

Years ago the railways dominated freight and travel. Over the years they lost much of their business to airlines, trucking companies and bus lines. The railways could have kept all that business; they lost it because somebody at a board meeting said: 'Our business is trains'. If they had said: 'Our business is freight and travel', then today the railways might own the airlines, trucking companies and bus lines. By making their goal one particular method they missed many opportunities. Similarly, many who work with young people would say: 'Our business is coffee-shops or camps or youth clubs'. When they think of their goal as a method they run the risk of being irrelevant to the young people they claim to serve. The method must never become the goal.

A BIBLICAL GOAL

What is our primary goal in Christian youth ministry?

In Colossians 1:28, Paul stated his goal in ministry in these words:

So we preach Christ to everyone. With all possible wisdom we warn and teach them *in order to bring each one into God's presence as a mature individual in union with Christ* (GNB).

Paul's goal in ministry was to present *every person mature in Christ.* The goal of Christian youth ministry should be to *present every young person mature in Christ.*The goal is not to run programs or use methods, because they are merely tools we use to achieve the goal of leading young people to maturity in Christ. When the goal is maturity in Christ the youth leader is set free to use any method which achieves that goal. Neither is the goal to hold young people within the fellowship of the church; that is a by-product of leading young people to maturity in Christ.

Now there may be all kinds of secondary goals. Goals may be set to contact so many new young people. Some youth leaders set evangelism goals. There are teaching goals where leaders identify certain things which they wish young people to learn. There might be goals for numerical growth or for up-grading the quality of the program. Numerous secondary goals can be adopted but they must all be subsumed under the one goal of leading young people to maturity in Christ.

This challenges the way we think about youth ministry because youth ministry is not only happening where there is a youth program. It is quite possible to have a youth program where hundreds of young people attend smoothly organised activities and yet no-one is led to maturity in Christ. On the other hand a church may lack an organised youth group, so that people say it has no youth ministry; yet, through personal relationships, young people are led to maturity in Christ.

WHAT IS MATURITY IN CHRIST?

The following chapters discuss how to contact unchurched young people, evangelise them and lead them on into spiritual maturity. At this point in the book it is helpful to consider where the whole process of youth ministry is heading. What are we finally trying to achieve in young people's lives? What do we mean by maturity in Christ?

Think again . . .

What are the qualities that make for a spiritually mature young person? 'Spiritual maturity' is one of those terms Christians use while assuming that everyone knows what they mean. But different Christians mean different things when they talk about maturity in Christ. To get a better idea of what you mean by spiritual maturity, fill in the following questionnaire.

Indicators of spiritual maturity

Number in order of priority the five characteristics that you believe would be the best indicators of spiritual maturity in young people. (Number five selections only.)

— Regular attendance at church activities.

— Self-control under pressure.

— Ability to interpret Scripture.

— Wears appropriate dress for church services.

— Punctuality.

— Makes perceptive comments about Christian doctrine.

— Joyfulness.

— Encourages others to live for Christ.

— Ability to assess the Christian standards of peers.

— A reflective, thoughtful personality.

— Commitment to a particular Christian activity.
— Generosity.
— Loyalty to Christian peers.
— Desire for holy living.
— Ability to preach a good message.
— A daily devotional pattern.
— A quiet manner.
— Patience with unreasonable parents.
— Regards other Christian young people with honour.
— Willingness to accept others.
— A concern for the work of a Christian group overseas.
— Pours oil on troubled waters.
— Reads the Authorised Version of the Bible.
— Never goes to the movies.
— Claims to pray regularly and at length.
— Helps others with their homework.
— Responded to an appeal to rededicate his life to Christ.
— Reads lots of Christian books.
— Tries to develop their gifts.
— Prays publicly in prayer meetings.

I have found that different youth leaders choose quite different characteristics when they do the above exercise. Some choose those characteristics that emphasise devotional life—Bible reading and prayer. Others emphasise loving relationships. Another group concentrates on obeying the rules. Some approach the matter theologically and emphasise qualities like skill in interpreting scripture. Another group again give great weight to an interest in mission or service while others emphasise emotional control.

Maturity in Christ in practice means quite different things to different youth leaders. To complicate the matter further, most of these youth leaders can quote Bible verses to support their view. It is important that we examine our own views and ask ourselves whether our priorities in Christian living really are the most important. Our view of Christian maturity needs to be the result of careful thought and not just assumptions. It will have a big bearing on the sort of young people we develop.

More than involvement

Maturity in Christ goes beyond doing Christian things. It is possible to have great skill in interpreting the Bible and yet disregard what it teaches. Involvement in Christian activity is not, of itself, a measure of maturity. Paul wrote to the Corinthians about people who do Christian work for the wrong motives. Jesus spoke of people who prophesied, performed miracles and cast out demons in the name of Christ and yet are not even Christians (Matthew 7:22). The fact that young people are active in Christian service, does not mean they are mature.

The same thing applies to attendance. While commitment to the corporate expression of faith that is found in church life may be an expression of spiritual maturity, we should not settle for mere attendance. There are many Christians who are quite happy as long as the young people show up at church functions. They think that as long as the young people are in the fold they are all right. As long as they make a 'decision', get confirmed or baptised, attend services, dress properly, make the right noises and don't do anything particularly anti-social then everything is fine.

Maturity in Christ, however, is not merely a matter of performing religious activities, no matter how sincerely they are practised. Spiritual maturity affects the whole life of a person, in its every aspect. Most Christians know this is true but often we don't operate this way.

Peter had been self-centred, materialistic and conceited for years but this never seemed to concern many of the Christians in his church. When he was about seventeen he dropped out of church and then people began to be concerned. The youth leader visited him and he began to attend church again. Some weeks later, his parents said to the youth leader 'Peter's going great. He's got a girlfriend in the youth group now so he goes to church all the time.' The youth leader could not observe any change in Peter's attitude and sometime later Peter dropped out again—this time, permanently. It is interesting how often we think the job is done simply because young people attend. Peter was not going great'; he was just going to church. Maturity in Christ is much more than that.

My priorities in spiritual maturity

The qualities that I regard as the most important to strive for in young people are outlined below. My choice of these qualities is, of course, influenced greatly by my own experience of life. Others would choose differently. I am not speaking of the sum total of my view of spiritual maturity, but of priorities that I can act upon in practical ways in youth ministry. They are:

(a) An understanding of the gospel. It is most important that young people base their acceptance with God on what Christ has done for them in his life, death and resurrection.

(b) Commitment. 'Be concerned above everything else with the Kingdom of God and with what he requires of you' (Matthew 6:33 GNB). Young people are called to submit to

the rule of Christ. As Christians they must be committed to Jesus Christ and to righteous living.

(c) The fruit of the Spirit. Spiritual maturity must be reflected in relationships with others. Galatians 5:22–23 sums up much of what is required: 'The fruit of the Spirit is love, joy, peace, patience, kindness, goodness, faithfulness, gentleness and self-control'.

(d) The servant attitude. Philippians 2 teaches that we should all have the servant attitude of Christ. Young people need to learn in the pressures of life that we are at our greatest when we are servants. We must serve our Christian brothers and sisters and the world at large. This involves the development and application of spiritual gifts.

(e) A devotional life. I believe the spiritually mature young person will develop a regular practice of Bible reading and prayer. Communication is basic in any relationship.

If you don't agree with my list of priorities, write your own. The process of identifying the specific qualities that you most want to see develop in young people's lives will help give your ministry more direction.

THE EXPRESSION OF MATURITY VARIES FROM PERSON TO PERSON

Once you have identified the qualities you are aiming for in young people, you must be careful to avoid a stereotyped approach to young people. They are not all the same and they will express their Christianity in different ways. What will be easy for some will be impossible for others. Some Christians greatly discourage young people by placing unrealistic expectations on them.

Three helpful principles

(a) The expression of maturity is related to age and experience

Philippians 3:12-16 teaches that the spiritually mature Christian is not someone who has arrived at a certain spiritual state but one who is involved in a growth process. Paul writes: 'Straining forward to what is ahead, I press on towards the goal'. There is no concept of having arrived: maturity means to be growing. If my maturity is not greater now than it was twelve months ago I am immature. Therefore a spiritually mature sixteen year old will be very different to a mature forty year old.

I well remember being in a meeting of church elders when complaints were raised about some of the things the young people in the church were doing. (This is not an unusual situation for youth leaders to find themselves in.) On this occasion the complaints turned out to be quite frivolous. The biggest complaint was that after the hall had been cleaned up somebody had left the dishmop (used for washing up) sitting on the floor. (I managed to conceal my initial reaction of 'Oh, no, not the dishmop!'.) I said to the men in that meeting: 'I knew many of you when you were teenagers and I saw how you behaved. You did not display anything like the level of maturity that you expect of the young people in this church'. Later one of them admitted that their expectations were unreasonable.

When Jesus was a child he was a perfect child. But he was still a child—he was not a miniature adult in a child's body. At thirteen Jesus was a perfect teenager: but he was not the same as he was at thirty. Jesus was always perfect, but his perfection changed expression as he grew up. So it is with spiritual maturity: its expression changes with age, experience and the developmental stages of life. One of the most discouraging things for young people is when adults expect of them a level of maturity that is beyond them. We must accept them as they are with all their relative immaturity, yet point them in the direction of spiritual maturity.

(b) The expression of maturity is related to gifts and abilities

At sixteen, Jason had a magnetic personality, smooth speech and a quick mind beyond his years. He was also keen to share his faith, having led three of his friends to Christ and brought another five to the youth group. David, the youth leader, was delighted: he continually talked about Jason and encouraged everyone else to be like him and tell all their friends about Jesus.

While all this was going on, Suzi and a few others seemed to withdraw. Suzi was an ordinary girl who had been keen to serve the Lord. She was always so reliable and willing to do those behind the scenes jobs. But now she seemed to lose interest. Suzi was not jealous of Jason nor had she reneged on her decision to follow Jesus. She had simply lost confidence and wondered whether she was any use at all to God. Suzi was a shy girl with average intelligence and poor communication skills. She had prayed earnestly that God would make her like Jason but it did not happen. Without realising it, David was giving her the message that the people God uses are outgoing, intelligent communicators—like Jason. To put that sort of expectation on someone who is shy and has poor communication skills has a devastating effect.

All Christians should do what they can to evangelise others. But the Bible teaches that some have a gift of evangelism. David was expecting someone who does not have the gift of evangelism to perform like someone who does. It was good to encourage the youth group to be like Jason. But in what sense could they be like Jason? They could not all exercise the gift of evangelism, although they could all be witnesses. They could all exercise the gifts and abilities God has given them. As it turned out, the youth group were being encouraged to exercise, not their gifts, but Jason's gift. When this happens, young people often respond like Suzi: they become frustrated and discouraged from serving God with the gifts he *has* given them.

David could have handled the whole thing quite differently. While encouraging all the young people to use their gifts, he could have commended Suzi in her serving as well as Jason in his evangelism. Suzi could have been encouraged to build relationships with non-Christians and to do what she could to influence them for Christ. In this she could learn from Jason, but she should never have been expected to evangelise like Jason. God had simply not equipped her for that sort of service.

Biblical knowledge is another area in which we discourage young people. There is no question that we should teach young people the message of the Bible, teach them to read it for themselves and encourage them to study it. However, it must be remembered that God has given people different levels of intelligence and different ways of thinking and this has nothing to do with their spiritual maturity. Some people have poor memories and will find it very difficult to remember scripture. Some have a limited ability to interpret literature while others are not good readers. These factors will affect how people use the Bible but they have little to do with spiritual maturity. They relate to qualities people have whether or not they are even Christians.

This is important because there is a tendency to treat the person with more Bible knowledge as more mature. Such knowledge may well be a sign of maturity; however, it also has a lot to do with intelligence. But what about the young person who does not have that sort of intelligence? There are many young people who think there is no place for them in Christian service because they have been given to believe that the people God uses are Bible scholars and theologians and they know they don't have those sorts of skills. Yet sometimes these young people demonstrate the fruit of the Spirit far more than those who seem to know all the answers. Some Christians have been conned by the world. The world values people by their intelligence: we often do the same in religious matters.

A very discouraged young lady came to see me. Narelle was on the leadership team of a youth group but was giving it up believing she had little to offer. As we began to explore her concerns I discovered that Narelle was dyslexic. When other members of the leadership team talked about the Christian books they were reading and the Bible passages they were studying, Narelle felt distinctly inferior. This was not just because of her reading disability but because spiritual brownie-points seemed to be attached to such reading and studying. Narelle just could not do what some assumed all mature young Christians should do. With her permission I raised the matter with her youth leader. While he was unaware of her disability he expressed great admiration for the work Narelle did in the pastoral care of girls and in organisational work. Narelle did eventually drop out. Unknowingly, the group had taught her which gifts really count and she knew she did not have them.

All gifts count to God. Care should be taken to affirm all gifts and to avoid fostering an expectation that all Christians should be able to do a particular thing. Young people should be encouraged to read and study their Bibles. But they should not be given the message that everyone can and ought to be a theologian and, that if you are not, you are of little use to God. Above all, it is important to emphasise the application of the scriptures to daily life. While learning the scriptures is important, it is more important that young people live by what they know. Maturity in Christ is not a matter of knowledge in the head but of qualities to be lived out. Faithfulness and obedience are required of all, regardless of gifts. This puts everyone on level ground because, regardless of ability, the Holy Spirit can grow his fruit on any believer.

(c) Maturity has its ups and downs

Even mature people behave immaturely sometimes. Sometimes young people will let themselves down and let their youth leader down too. It is helpful to think of the difference between the climate and the weather. The *climate* of an area consists of an average of the weather which occurs over a period of time. The *weather* is what is happening now. You can get a good day in a bad climate and you can have terrible storms in a good climate. Young people are like that. With the stresses on young people they will have their storms. But when monitoring their growth, look not at the storms but at the overall climate of their lives. Be prepared to ride out the storms while striving for an overall improvement in the climate.

We shall return

In the final chapter we will return to this theme of maturity in Christ when we consider 'Developing spiritual maturity in young people'. In this chapter we have considered the goal of youth work. The rest of the book is on how to get there.

▶ ▶

2

how will you get there?

A STRATEGY FOR YOUTH MINISTRY

▶ ▶

A youth group I once led grew very large. Quite a number of youth leaders asked me if they could come to some of the activities to see what had made the group grow. Having seen the group many of these people were obviously disappointed. Some remarked that the activities were really no different to those done by other groups.

This was obviously a problem to them because they assumed we had some secret little attraction that was an irresistible drawcard for young people. They were working on the false assumption that youth ministry is built on gimmicks and fast ideas. I well remember one of them asking in amazement: 'But how do you get them through the doors?' It took six months or perhaps a year to get each one through the doors. It took months of love and care for them as individuals, combined with a strategic approach to drawing them into the youth group; to build those young people into that group.

Good programming is important but it is not the foundation. Effective youth ministry is built on quality relationships and sound strategy—*not* on activities or meetings.

We have already seen that a biblical goal for youth ministry is to lead young people to maturity in Christ. In this chapter we will consider a strategy which can help the youth leader organise the youth program so that every young person can be reached at their present level of interest yet led in the direction of Christian maturity. First, however, we will consider an important principle.

BALANCE

'I was only trying to share the gospel . . .'

Wayne was a keen and very likeable church youth leader. He was particularly keen on evangelism and so he started a coffee-shop in an attempt to reach the young people of his district for Christ. The youth group was expected to run the coffee-shop—it would be *their* outreach in the community. It was decided to open it on both Friday and Saturday nights to make the most of the opportunity.

All seemed to go fairly well for the first couple of months. Young people came to the coffee-shop and Wayne had opportunities to use his evangelistic gift. He had little time, though, for anything else. Then the problems began in the youth group.

Keith and Richard both left to join another youth group. They said 'We don't even feel adequate to explain our faith to our school friends, let alone the kids who come to the coffee-shop. Besides, we're really learning a lot at the Bible studies at our new youth group.' Fifteen year old Julie refused to go to youth group saying that it was no fun anymore. Two boys from church families were charged with underage drinking. When the non-Christians who came to the coffee-shop heard this they had a good laugh.

To make matters worse Mrs Scott, who never seemed to like anyone from Wayne's family, complained that this might never have happened if the youth leader had spent more time with the church young people. At a church members' meeting some parents called for a new youth leader while others pressed for youth Bible studies and socials.

Like many youth leaders, Wayne ran into problems because his program was unbalanced: one aspect of ministry was emphasised at the expense of others. In Wayne's case in emphasising evangelism, he neglected other needs of the group. Without a Bible study or discipleship program the Christians were not equipped for effective evangelism. Spiritual and relationship problems were also more likely to occur. Furthermore, some members of the youth group and their parents became dissatisfied with the emphasis and undermined the leadership. All these factors combined to erode the evangelistic effort. By being so concerned about evangelism that other needs were neglected, Wayne actually weakened the evangelistic outreach. Unbalanced programs usually run into problems. If Wayne's program was unbalanced with a bias towards Bible studies or socials similar problems would be likely to emerge. All needs of a youth group are integrated: if one is neglected it affects the others.

How do we lose our balance?

There are a number of reasons why such imbalances occur. Wayne's problem was that he had a strong interest in a particular type of ministry and projected that onto the group. That can happen with Bible study, sport, all sorts of things. Laziness can also be a cause of imbalance. It may seem easier to regurgitate the same old activities that meet limited needs than to do the work required to meet the variety of needs in a youth group. Often imbalances occur while trying to correct a previous imbalance. Wayne's youth group had a bias towards evangelism at the expense of Bible study and they did very little besides run a coffee-shop for a long time. Once the imbalance was recognised it would not be uncommon for the group to have nothing but Bible studies for a long time. Thus, in an effort to correct one imbalance, another situation of imbalance is set up that will only create further problems down the line. Some youth programs are like pendulums that swing from one state of imbalance to another.

Lack of forward planning can also create imbalances. When youth leaders plan activities week-to-week without reference to a longer-term plan they easily lose sight of what is being neglected and what is being over-emphasised. Many youth leaders are so consumed with pulling together an activity for this Friday night that they never stop to look at the larger picture. Unless the long-term program is planned in advance, the youth leader will tend to organise activities that are easy to do or that give the leader himself most gratification rather than those activities that meet the needs of the group. Ideally a youth program should be structured so that all needs are being met all the time and no one need is being emphasised at the expense of others.

What are the needs?

What are the needs of young people that need to be addressed in a youth program?

- All young people, and especially those who are not Christians, need the gospel. Therefore evangelism is needed.
- To evangelise young people, they must first be contacted.

- Christian young people need to be taught the Christian faith and should be encouraged to pray and to serve.
- As they become more established, those with leadership potential need leadership training.
- It is important for all young people to have the fun and fellowship that social activities provide.
- Christian young people should also consider their responsibilities to try to meet the needs of the world. In particular it is important that a concern be developed for missions and for the socially disadvantaged.

Therefore we can identify eight elements that should be included in a youth program:

1. Contacting.
2. Evangelism.
3. Bible study.
4. Prayer.
5. Social activity (fun, friendship and relaxation).
6. Social concern for the disadvantaged.
7. Missions (a concern for needs beyond the immediate situation.)
8. Leadership training.

Now some of these elements can be combined in the one activity. For example, Bible study and prayer can be effectively organised together in the one Bible study program. Missions input could be included in the same program from time to time. Social activities that provide fun and fellowship have potential for contacting young people who are not Christians if they are consciously put to use in that way. In other words these eight elements are *things that should happen in a youth program:* they do not necessarily mean eight different *activities.*

All these elements should be included in a youth program in a balanced way. This does not mean that each element should be granted equal time; however, during each year there should be activities that satisfy the requirements of each element.

Thinking ahead

In practice this means that we need to determine the frequency each element deserves and plan the program accordingly. Here are a couple of examples of how this could be done:

Example 1. This youth group has enough leaders and the young people have enough time for the group to meet twice per week. They have one evangelistic activity per week; one Bible study per week; a social/contacting event once per month; three activities per year to meet the needs of the disadvantaged and one leadership training weekend per year.

Example 2. This group has decided to meet once per week. Every second week there is a Bible study geared for Christians. The alternate weeks are geared for young people outside the church circle with a social/contacting event once every fortnight and an evangelistic event every alternate fortnight. Therefore the pattern every four weeks will be:

- Social/contacting.
- Bible study.
- Evangelism.
- Bible study.

On top of this they have two activities per year to meet the needs of the disadvantaged, and a leadership training segment is attached to the monthly youth committee meeting.

Both of the above groups have been organised quite differently to reflect different needs and emphases. Yet in both groups all of the eight essential elements of a youth program are included in a balanced way.

Feeling the pulse

The way each youth group puts it together will need to be determined in terms of the context in which the group finds itself. Relevant factors include the availability of people and resources and the needs, opportunities and pressures in the community.

For example it will obviously take more time, and probably leaders, to operate two time slots each week than one. It is also likely to cost more financially. Do we have the leaders, time and money to sustain two time slots? In some places most young people may have time to attend only once per week while in other places, like areas with high unemployment, they have plenty of time.

Some groups will need to allocate more time to the needs of the disadvantaged than other groups because they live in areas of high social need. In some places there is little entertainment available for young people and they come to Christian activities fairly easily. In such a district a youth group may not need to have many (or any) contacting activities.

No matter what the group's special characteristics, balance is the key. If in time it is found that a particular need is not being met, the whole program can be adjusted to meet that need in a balanced way. Be careful, however, not to overcompensate and create a new imbalance.

THE THREE CIRCLE STRATEGY

It is possible to incorporate all the above eight elements in a youth program, yet find that they are not working together towards a common goal. A youth program needs more than balance. It needs direction—and that comes from a strategy which pulls all the elements together.

Some of these elements are not so easy to integrate, however, especially if you are diligent in evangelism. Evangelism usually creates problems because it brings together people of different motivation and backgrounds. It is one thing to minister to either the committed or the uncommitted; how do we minister to both in the one group? How do we introduce newcomers to church without scaring them away? The following strategy addresses these issues.

FIGURE 1

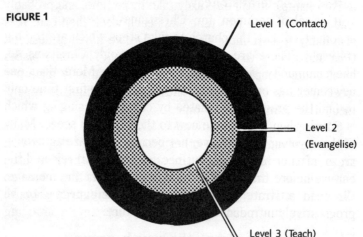

Level 1 (Contact)

Level 2 (Evangelise)

Level 3 (Teach)

The circles represent different levels of religious sub-culture

We Christians have a sub-culture of our own. We can imagine that people who are totally removed from our sub-culture are outside the level 3 circle. As we move closer to the centre of the circles the sub-culture becomes more removed from that of society at large. When non-Christians enter our world they often feel out of place. Yet often

Christians are not sensitive to this: they expect these people to take one big step when a number of smaller steps will do. Christians make this mistake especially with time. Instead of allowing young people time to come to Christ they often evangelise in short-term projects like weekend camps and youth rallies. This sort of time frame is too quick for most people. We need to work with most young people consistently over a long period of time before they will come to Christ. We need a strategy that facilitates such long-term, evangelistic contact. Camps, special events and rallies can be useful in evangelism but for maximum effect they need to be part of a long-term strategy.

It is also common for Christians to expect people unconnected with the church to take steps which are too big culturally. There are many things that only Christians do, like community singing and public prayer. More than one newcomer has come to a youth group for the first time only to find the program dominated by community singing which is utterly alien to someone new to the Christian scene. Many of these young people leave, not because they are antagonistic to Jesus or his gospel, but because they have rejected the culture before they have had a chance to hear the message. We need a strategy that allows for young people to be progressively introduced to church culture.

The circles represent the youth group

They are a way to visualise three different types of young people that might be found in a youth group. Level 1 represents young people who are prepared to have social contact with the youth group but are not prepared or not ready to take the relationship any further. Level 2 represents those who have had enough contact with the group to have confidence to regularly attend activities where the gospel is communicated. Level 3 represents Christian young people who will willingly attend activities for Bible study and prayer. They are the core of the youth group or 'core group'.

The circles represent three levels of ministry

They represent a way to organise the youth group. We can organise activities on three levels. The goal of level 1 activities is contact. The activity is designed to attract new contacts into the group and consolidate old contacts. Level 1 events can often double as social events because fun activities usually have great potential to attract newcomers. Usually there would be no message presented in a formal way (although informal sharing of the gospel may take place).

The purpose at this level is to introduce new contacts to the youth group and to Christian young people in a non-threatening environment. Hopefully they will see that Christians are not really weird: that they are ordinary people who enjoy having fun together. Of course it is important that the activities planned should actually be enjoyable! At these activities some of these people should start to identify with Christians and begin to want to be like them.

There are some young people who will come directly into evangelistic activities and we should always be willing to accomodate them. But we must recognise that these are exceptions: most young people will not come to activities where the gospel is declared until we have already broken down the barriers and won their confidence. This is the purpose of level 1 activities. So instead of trying to get teenagers from the community at large directly into evangelistic activities the process is broken down into two steps that they are more likely to take.

Promotion of level 1 activities should concentrate on those who are outside all the circles (i.e. young people from society at large who have not been to a youth group activity before).

The goal is not just to see a lot of young people coming along but to make new contacts and consolidate old ones. Sometimes the effectiveness of these activities is reduced when lots of Christians from other youth groups are invited. The activity may be well attended but the goal of contacting will not be achieved. In a later chapter we will consider the types of activities that make for good contacting.

Level 2 activities are designed for evangelism. This does not mean that they have to be heavy evangelistic rallies; a level 2 activity can be a fun program with a significant evangelistic input of, say, 15 minutes duration. The important thing is that these activities consistently and regularly present the message of the gospel to young people. Consistent, long-term exposure is far more effective than occasional, heavy pressure. It is 'the dripping of the tap that wears away the stone' while the heavy blast of the hose tends to wash the stone away entirely. Promotion of evangelistic activities concentrates on young people who have already been prepared through contact at level 1.

The goal of level 3 activities is the development of young people through teaching, Bible study, prayer and discipleship. These are core group activities and they serve the dual purpose of nurture for new and young Christians as well as equipping and motivating all to minister to their peers. Just as level 2 people are recruited from level 1, so level 3 people are recruited from level 2. Youth leaders should always be on the lookout for young people who are showing a keen interest in the gospel in order to introduce them to level 3. Once they are established in the core group they can then be introduced to the regular worship service of the local church.

How it all fits together: James' story

James was invited to youth group by friends at school. He was a bit reluctant to go to a Christian function but it sounded like fun and he was assured that no one would pressurise or embarrass him. The first youth group night he went to was a Sock Hop: a crazy night of fifties music, dance and activities. Not long after that there was a sports night in a local hall. James had never seen games like the ones he played that night. Like most young guys he was totally unaware of the fun ideas that are so readily available in youth group resource books today. He simply put it all down to a brilliant youth leader.

Then James went to a weekend camp. Games on the beach featured, climaxing in an all-in water and flour fight. Water bombs were made with balloons and flour was poured into little paper bags. James recalls how all of these activities shattered his preconceived ideas of Christians. Although they were serious about their faith, James recalls that these Christians experienced 'no-holds-barred fun'.

Eventually James started to go to a monthly coffee-shop run by the youth group. He knew that a speaker would share a gospel message but his resistance to that had now broken down. At the coffee-shop he enjoyed the Christian bands and drama, and he learned from the speakers. But most of all he enjoyed the people. This is what kept him going to the group. The activities were good, but more importantly, the people were genuine people who really loved him.

James decided to become a follower of Jesus and began to go to the youth group Bible studies. This was a big step for James because he was self-conscious about praying and he knew that Bible studies involved group prayer. He knew that he would not have to pray but he felt awkward all the same. Slowly James eased into the Bible studies and became a solid member of the core group. It was not long before he was bringing his non-Christian friends along to the youth group.

Step by step

Instead of trying to introduce young people to the church in one big step, this strategy breaks down the process into several small steps. As commitment grows, young people have the opportunity to involve themselves in more activities that both express and promote greater commitment.

As they move on from level 1 to levels 2 and 3 they should not cease to attend the level 1 events. Hopefully they will still come to social and contact events but with a different motivation and purpose. Where they formerly came chiefly for pleasure and social contact, they should now also have a goal of helping their peers come to Christ.

The numbers of people attending at level 1 should as a rule be much higher than at level 3. This is because a level 3 activity should demand much greater commitment. If the same number of people attend level 3 as attend level 1, something is wrong. Either the group is not contacting effectively, resulting in level 1 being too small, or it is not discipling its Christians strongly enough so that level 3 is too large.

Effective level 3 events tend to naturally separate 'the sheep from the goats' so there should be a progressive drop off in attendance through the levels. We might expect that a youth group that has 80 members at level 1 might have 50 at level 2 and 25 at level 3. Nobody sorts out young people into the various levels. If the program is run so that level 1 consistently contacts, level 2 consistently evangelises and level 3 consistently teaches, the young people will sort themselves out into the appropriate levels.

It must be understood that each activity does more than achieve its own goals. Every activity contributes to the overall process of taking people from the general community and bringing them into the inner circle of the Christian fellowship. It is not just a matter of organising activities at which certain Christian ideas are communicated. It is also a matter of absorbing people further into the love, fellowship and care of the Christian church. This strategy accepts people where they are but always invites them to come further.

Don't freak them out

Exposure to church culture is kept at a minimum at level 1. In fact a level 1 activity should be the kind of activity that a high school could sponsor. Church culture is progressively introduced through levels 2 and 3. Every effort should be made to prevent purely cultural practices from becoming a hindrance to the gospel. Perhaps community singing should not be introduced until level 3. This strategy allows all young people to be regularly part of the youth group at whatever level they are prepared to accept for as long as they need to stay at that level. It gives young people the time to progress at their own rate. It gives the youth leaders time to sow the seed of the gospel and nurture the crop until harvest.

It might look the same but ...

An approach which is very different to the three circle strategy is represented in the following diagram.

What we have here is three totally separate youth groups in the one church. One group is purely a social group while a second group has an evangelistic program. A third group meets together for Bible study. On the surface this may appear to be similar to the three level strategy but in reality it is nothing like it. The group dynamics are completely different.

FIGURE 2

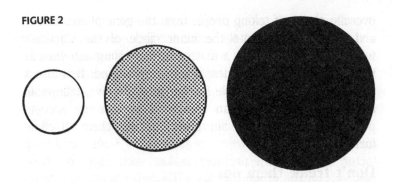

For the three level strategy to really work, the Bible study group must be the core group at every level of operation. They must be totally involved in contacting/social activities as well as the evangelistic activities. There must be one group operating at three levels, not three different groups with separate activities. One group must reach out into the community to contact, evangelise and teach.

If they are not in fact one group there is unlikely to be a flow on from one group to the next. The social group may contact new people, but these contacts are unlikely to come to the evangelistic events because that involves joining a new group. The evangelistic group may see people won for Christ but converts are unlikely to move on to the Bible study group. A lot of effort may be made and many young people may attend but in the end very few actually join the fellowship of the church.

This situation can occur even when the youth leaders want the three level strategy to operate. It is fundamentally a matter of attitude and commitment. I have seen youth groups where people were continually being converted and this was mainly as a result of the witness of the Christian core. Yet other groups, where well organised, evangelistic programs are produced by the leaders, seem to achieve little because the core group don't want to reach others in the community. They want the group for themselves; they don't welcome newcomers and will sometimes deliberately exclude them. If at least some of the Christian young people are not willing to involve themselves so as to be a core group on all levels, the three level strategy will not function.

This is usually a spiritual problem and cannot be solved by mere organisation; however organisational issues can be a factor. If the youth program makes such excessive time demands on the group that keen, Christian young people do not have the time to be involved in all three levels, they will have to choose between them. We must weigh up whether adding to the program will mean more effective ministry. Sometimes it makes the whole youth group less productive. It takes careful and wise monitoring to keep the core group functioning effectively.

CHRISTIAN PEER PRESSURE

As I noted at the start of this chapter, the effectiveness of youth ministry is largely determined by the quality of relationships between people. Of crucial importance are relationships between Christians and people who are not Christians. The three circle strategy hinges not only on catering for different interest levels in activities, but on exposing those who are not committed to Christ to the Christian core. The friendships that result are just as much a part of the youth ministry as the organised activities at which Christian teaching is communicated. In fact, developing that ministry of Christian young people to their peers is what youth ministry is really all about. The role of adults who are involved is rather like that of the coach of a sports team: training, facilitating, encouraging. This contrasts with much of what passes for youth ministry, where young people passively look on as adults decide everything, do everything and say everything.

What exactly is this ministry of young people to their peers? I am thinking of attentive, personal caring that goes on all through the week, and not just when the youth group meets. When Christian teenagers share the gospel with their peers, show loving acceptance of them or pastorally care for them, it can have an immense impact.

'I saw how God wanted me to behave'

It is well known that peer pressure is very powerful during adolescent years. This is often assumed to be a bad thing. In fact it is neutral; peer pressure can produce good as well as bad results. Just as peer pressure can encourage young people to take drugs or have sex outside marriage, so pressure from different peers can encourage them to say no to drugs, adopt high moral standards and perhaps even read their Bibles and attend church services. Peer pressure can motivate young people to become Christians and it can encourage genuine behavioural change.

Robert's story, below, demonstrates the effect of the peer group in encouraging positive change.

When I became a Christian I began to learn more about the Christian life. One of the first things I realised was how different I was to my friends in the youth group at church. One of the most noticeable things was my swearing. Even before I was a Christian I noticed that my Christian friends at school did not swear. I believed it was wrong but I did not do anything about it until after I joined the youth group.

That group seemed to have an unusual effect on me. On the one hand the group did not reject me because of my bad language. They accepted me just as I was: bad language and all. They did not put any direct pressure on me to change. I don't remember anyone in the youth group telling me not to swear. But in the conversation of guys and girls in the youth group I saw how God wanted me to talk. God used their example to help and encourage me to change.

The more I mixed with the youth group the more I was challenged to change because my language stood out as so different to theirs. I prayed to God to help me stop swearing and I was continually encouraged by my friends who did not swear. I felt happier with myself, more a part of the group and, most importantly, that God had helped me to change. At the time it seemed like a real achievement in Christian living.

Youth leaders need to place a high priority on building a core group that supports and demonstrates the principles being taught, and thus exerts a Christian peer group pressure. The Christian gospel can then be clearly seen to involve more than abstract ideas. When others see the gospel in flesh and blood in the lives of young people, they will see that it is powerful and relevant. Having a group of authentically Christian young people with which others will want to identify is more than half the battle. Chapter 6 looks at how to build such a group.

The effects of a properly trained and mobilised core are illustrated by the following diagram.

The core reach out drawing other young people from one level to the next. They bring them to level 1, then from level 1 to level 2 then to level 3. In doing this they are not just inviting others to activities, but evangelising them through their relationships and encouraging change in attitudes, beliefs and behaviour. It has often been said that the best

FIGURE 3

person to evangelise a teenager is another teenager. This effect is multiplied when young people evangelise in peer groups.

United we stand

Emma illustrates another benefit of Christian peer pressure. Emma finds it a struggle to read her Bible and pray regularly. But she is encouraged to persevere, knowing that the other girls in the youth group also struggle yet try hard to have a daily quiet time. Some days it doesn't work out, but Emma is sure that if it were not for her Christian friends her Bible would not get opened very much at all. Emma also feels left out when her classmates have their drinking parties and sometimes she is tempted to join in, but knowing that she is accepted by her Christian youth group helps her to say 'no'.

Christian peer group pressure can counteract the peer group pressure of the surrounding community. This is illustrated by Figure 4. When others put on the pressure to cheat, disobey parents or behave selfishly, the peer pressure of the Christian group helps young people to resist, and reinforces and encourages righteous behaviour, values and beliefs. But Christian peer pressure is able to do far more than merely oppose non-Christian peer pressure. God is more powerful than other forces in the world and he is able to work through his young people to win others for the Kingdom of God.

FIGURE 4

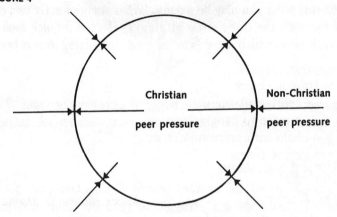

Christian

peer pressure

Non-Christian

peer pressure

It's quality that counts ... and grows

There is an important principle here: as a rule you do not build quality from quantity; rather, you build quantity from quality. The mistake that youth leaders often make is to assemble large numbers of young people and then try to build Christianity into them without first developing a small core group of Christians. Now that approach does sometimes work out, but such groups are dominated by the values and behavioural norms of the community at large, and these will usually outweigh the Christian message which the leader is trying to teach. In other words, where there is no active

Christian core there is no strong model of adolescent Christianity for other young people to identify with.

Whether or not the gospel is declared, ultimately young people are more likely to be like the others they can see and know than the Christians they only hear about. If possible it is preferable to start small and get real Christian discipleship happening in a core group, then build on that.

WHERE DO WE START?

At this point you may be asking, 'What sorts of activities can I use with the three circle strategy?'. Here is a quick look at some ideas which are described more fully later in this book.

Weekly/regular
- Drop-in centre
  — sport/crafts/music
  — a place to hang around
  — help with homework/study
- Sporting teams

One offs

Fun & games
- Rumble (crazy indoor games)
- Crazy auction
- VW pack
- Fashion parade
- Crazy fashion parade

Monster mess
- Mud bowl
- Pillow fight
- Custard fight
- War games (flour bombs, water bombs)

Music, dance & drama
- Dance
- Bush dance
- 50's night
- Sock hop
- Concert
- Talent quest
- Theatre sports
- Set up your own movie theatre

Food
- Barbecue
- Progressive dinner

- Youth banquet
- World's largest banana split/jelly/spaghetti
- Bad taste dinner
- Luau
- Hawaiian night

Out & about

- Scavenger hunt
- Sounds crazy (scavenger hunt to record sounds)
- Elephant hunt
- Wild goose chase
- Mission impossible
- Boat cruise
- Bus trip

- Spy v spy
- Person find
- An all night series of activities (e.g. concert, bowling, skating, video, breakfast)

Let's party

- Candid camera party (slides and photos of youth group as children)
- Fancy dress party
- Masquerade party
- Pool party
- Skating party

Ideas for level 2 activities

Many of the ideas in the Level 1 list can be used effectively for Level 2 activities if evangelistic content is also included. Make sure the evangelistic segment integrates naturally with the rest of the event — don't tack it on at the end.

Specific methods of youth evangelism

Chapter 5 deals with this at length, but here are four methods for now:

- Home meetings (meet in a living room for games, discussion and supper)
- Coffee shops
- Youth rallies
- Camps

▶ ▶

3

making it happen

IMPLEMENTING THE STRATEGY

▶ ▶

How do you make the youth group happen? This chapter discusses how to pull together the strategy outlined in the previous chapter and deal with issues that affect ministry on all levels. The chapter divides into two areas that concern youth leaders: managing people and organising programs.

MANAGING PEOPLE

Youth leaders should consider the following four issues as they manage the people in their youth groups.

1. Check your leadership style

The young people themselves must 'own' the youth group. If the kind of peer ministry that is described in chapter 2 is to take place, the Christian core must believe that the youth ministry is *their* work. For example, they must be confident that the evangelistic activities of the youth program are an expression of their faith and not just a series of meetings which have been imposed upon them and to which they are told to bring their friends. They must feel that they are the basic functioning unit of the youth program and that they are free to make their own statement to their peers through it.

Decisions, decisions

The degree to which this happens depends greatly on the style of the leaders. Leaders need to know the difference between guiding and imposing. If young people are to 'own' the program, they need to be empowered to make decisions that affect it. A leader needs skill to know what they should decide and what they should allow the young people to decide. Some decisions, of course, should be made by adult leaders. However youth leaders sometimes refuse to allow young people to make decisions that might in fact be better made by them.

For example, when one youth group wanted to run a contacting event, the leader insisted on having a barbecue at his home although most of the core group were keen to have a pool party at one of their homes. Now as long as the event achieves the goal of contacting, it does not really matter whether it happens at a pool party or a barbecue. This is a small decision that the youth group can make and it could make a great difference to how much the youth group 'own' the event and get behind it. This does not mean that youth leaders should not decide such issues. They often will and must. But youth leaders must carefully monitor how much the young people 'own' the program and must be willing to listen, adjust and change.

Wise youth leaders are keen for young people to make decisions and they have thought through what should be decided by them and what should be decided by leaders. As a general rule leaders should decide issues of broad strategy and direction, while young people are often quite capable of deciding many of the details of programs within the strategy.

Servants or stars

Leadership style often comes down to a question of the leader's goals and attitudes. Do we want young people to minister effectively to each other and to their peers or do we want them to be spectators of our ministry? Do we want to be servants or stars? Youth leaders who want to be stars tend to focus the program around themselves instead of young people. They design the program so that they are always the centre of attention. They run the games and do the talks even when others are available and they don't allow young people to work their way into these roles. This reduces the degree to which the young people 'own' the program. Good youth leaders aim to work young people into the forefront of the program and take a back seat themselves. Others are so much in the forefront that the casual observer might mistakenly think that the youth leader is not even running the program. Such involvement does not happen overnight; young people need to be trained for it and it may take months, even years. But good youth leaders head in this direction.

The leadership team who assist the youth leader must also 'own' the work. They must also share in decision making and the leader must train and facilitate them to encourage the young people in their ministry.

2. Delegate wisely

Clearly leaders need to delegate to young people and to their leadership team. Much has been written about delegation skills and there is no need to repeat such information in this book. However, beyond the skills themselves, there are important principles to consider regarding what and when to delegate to young people. Think about the following story . . .

It's 11:00 pm and thirty-three teenagers have all gone home. As youth leader Barbara drives home, she reflects on the evening. It was to have been an evangelistic program: a barbecue, followed by some games, music and a discussion through which the gospel was to be presented. The idea was that the Christians were to bring along their friends from outside the church. That part at least succeeded: there were at least fifteen newcomers that Barbara knew of, but something seemed to go awfully wrong when it came to sharing the gospel. At the barbecue the newcomers were left on their own with no one talking to them. Some did not even stay for the games. The games went well but the discussion was the real disappointment: it lacked direction and the discussion leader simply lost control.

Poor delegation was a major factor in these problems. The Christians would have been willing to talk to their friends during the barbecue, but they were too busy doing the jobs they had been delegated. Instead of talking to their friends they were cooking, preparing and serving food and washing up.

It is important that young people learn that sort of service—but not at a time like this. Avoid delegation that removes young people from face to face ministry with their peers. Usually parents or other adults can be found to do the cooking and other tasks. This is not to suggest that young people should never perform behind the scenes roles, but when we do delegate such roles to them, we must weigh up the consequences.

- *Principle 1:* Youth involvement in running an event needs to be balanced against their personal ministry to their peers.

There was another problem with Barbara's program: at strategic points it lacked quality. This was also related to delegation decisions. The plan was for someone to sing between the games and discussion. Sixteen year old Ryan sang and really made a mess of it. People were laughing for the wrong reason even before the discussion began.

Ryan was asked to sing because he was well liked at school. Barbara thought it would be good to involve him up front and he did have some talent. This is good thinking, but Ryan was simply not ready yet. Twenty-four year old Jane could have been invited to sing instead. The visitors would not have identified with her as much but she did have developed talent.

The discussion also went badly. It was led by Robert, one of the assistant youth leaders, and he was clearly out of his depth. Robert was allowed to lead the discussion because he felt that it was his turn and no-one had the heart to turn him down. Barbara thought it would be good experience for him. Robert was untrained and ill-prepared and he found out the hard way that discussions are not as easy as they look.

There are lots of good reasons for involving young people in the program: it is good training, newcomers are more likely to identify with young people and the youth group is more likely to 'own' the program. But these advantages have to be weighed up against the possible drop in the quality of the program that may be brought about through youth involvement.

- *Principle 2:* The need for youth participation in programs must be balanced against program quality.

The appropriate course of action will depend on the specific situation. While it is often better to sacrifice quality for youth involvement, sometimes it ends in disaster. Sometimes the young people involved are so capable that it is not an issue. The leaders must explore the question.

3. Keep control

Peer pressure discipline

Many youth leaders find discipline to be one of their most difficult tasks. How can we maintain control without becoming heavy-handed? The key to crowd control lies with the core group. If the Christian core are taught to set an acceptable standard of behaviour, most people who join at levels 1 or 2 will tend to conform. That is what most people do: whether they are at a hotel, school or party, they sense the standards and conform.

It is important then to teach the core group their role in establishing and maintaining control. They need to be regularly reminded that *they* set the standards for the whole group and that they must model that standard to others. They need to be taught what to do when somebody else behaves in an unacceptable way. For example, if the person next to them wants to talk when a speaker is speaking, teach them to avoid being drawn in and to say something like: 'Do you mind if we talk about this later, I really want to hear what Bob is saying'.

Discipline is thus a matter of applying peer pressure in a positive way. Most Christian young people appreciate this approach even though it puts the responsibility on them. They can see that this is far better than running the risk of their youth leader screaming at the friends they bring to youth group.

In any group, discipline will break down from time to time. This is often because the core has not been strong enough in setting an example. If the matter is serious enough, the leaders may need to take strong, direct action at the time. If it is not so serious, the leaders can choose to wait until the next time they have the core group together on their own.

To remind the core group of their responsibilities will usually improve behaviour through levels 1 and 2 as well.

Difficult young people

Some young people, usually a minority, will not respond to core group pressure. They will often behave badly elsewhere as well, e.g. home and school. It is better to deal with these young people in person and alone. Try to understand the conflicts and pressures that lie beneath the behaviour that you see on the surface. To deal with these issues you may need the help of someone with more expertise (and/or time). There is a limit to the number of troubled young people to whom you can give a lot of time.

With regard to the youth program, explain how difficult it is to lead the youth group when individuals don't cooperate. Avoid putting their ego on the line so that they have to lose face with the rest of the group to comply with what you want. Make it as easy as you can for them to cooperate.

If you have done your best and they are still disruptive, you may be left with no other option but to exclude them from the youth group. They could be suspended for a number of weeks or expelled altogether. Most youth leaders are reluctant to do this, but it is better than destroying the whole group. The mere threat of suspension will pull many such young people into line; however, don't threaten what you are not prepared to do.

4. Avoid attendance cycles

It has been observed that attendance at many youth groups goes in cycles. Over the years there are times of growth, followed by decline, followed by further periods of growth. Some suggest that such cycles are inevitable, but this is not the case. There are always reasons for growth and reasons for decline. Some of them are listed below.

- The changing population in a district may affect attendances. As families or young people leave or join a district, youth group attendances may be affected.

- Good leaders are replaced by inferior leaders who are unable to maintain the standard.

- There is a growth spurt because of the use of some new gimmick(s). But interest soon dies as there is no substance to maintain the group.

- Growth occurs through the exercise of good ministry principles combined with hard work. In time it is taken for granted: the ministry principles are compromised or the effort is no longer made. Decline sets in.

- Growth occurs among the older group members while the younger ones are neglected. This is illustrated below.

FIGURE 5

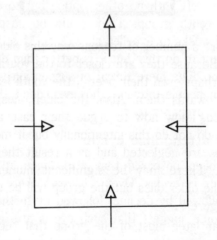

Figure 5, on page 50, represents a senior youth group catering for teenagers aged 15 to 19 years. The arrows indicate the way people flow through the youth group. They enter as they graduate from a more junior youth program (bottom arrow) or as they are contacted from the community (side arrows). They leave when they get too old for the group (top arrow).

Often cycles occur because the leaders concentrate on the older group members at the expense of the younger ones. The older members are shaded in Figure 6.

FIGURE 6

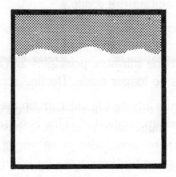

There are a number of reasons why this older group gets favoured. Because they are closer to the youth leaders' age (or are perhaps even their peers), the youth leaders tend to gravitate towards them. Also, the older ones, being more experienced, know how to argue their case and get their way. They do not do this intentionally but it means that the young ones are neglected and as a result their attendance drops off. There may be significant numerical growth amongst the older ones but the group will be short lived as seen in Figure 7.

One year later most of the group that received all the attention has left the youth group and two years later they

FIGURE 7

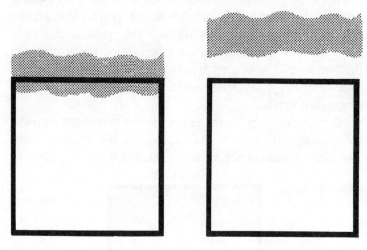

are all gone. It is quite common to find churches that once had dozens of young people and now have none. It was assumed that there would always be young people around, but when they grew up there were no younger ones to take their place. This can happen to any church that neglects its younger teenagers for just a few years.

Consider the difference it makes when the leaders are careful to not neglect the younger ones but ensure that they welcome and nurture them. Figure 8 shows the movement of this year's newcomers through the youth group.

By being careful not to neglect the youngest members of the youth group, the youth leaders will give themselves five years to work with each young person. If they are careful to do this every year they will avoid one of the major causes of cycles because they will always have new blood coming through.

FIGURE 8

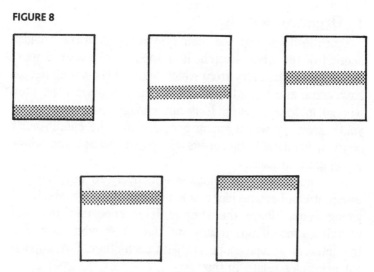

Another advantage is that by the time such young people reach their final year, they will have benefited from many years of training and should be able to make a greater contribution.

None of this is to suggest that the older members are to be neglected. We need to make sure that we are giving our greatest love and care equally to everyone, rather than allowing ourselves to serve the older members at the expense of the younger ones. But at the same time, it must always be a priority to settle newcomers into the group. This is not just because newcomers and younger ones need a relationship with the Lord and need the fellowship of the group but also because ultimately they are the long-term future of the youth group.

ORGANISING PROGRAMS

As well as managing people, youth leaders must also be able to organise programs. Much can be written on this subject but I want to confine my comments to three broad areas.

1. Organise broadly

Youth leaders must see their role in terms of the broader context of the whole church. It is important to bear in mind the children's ministry from which many of the young people have come and the adult ministries to which we hope they will go in future years. It is not enough merely to run a youth group to which young people come: the church must concern itself with the needs of people through the whole growing up process.

If a church fails to minister effectively to any one age group, it can become like a hole in a dam through which the young people leave the church. It is important that the church serves all age groups and that those who work with the different groups cooperate with each other. Two important principles relate to this.

Segregate into age groups

Twelve year olds are totally different to 18 year olds; it is not possible to meet the needs of both these age groups in the one group. Youth groups that try to reach everyone from 12 to 20 usually minister effectively only to the older ones or the younger ones—never both. Eighteen year olds need to discuss issues that twelve or thirteen year olds can't grapple with; content that is suitable for the younger ones will bore the older ones. Apart from content, 18 year olds are far more sophisticated than 12 or 13 year olds in the way they behave and also tend to be attracted to a different style of program.

It is best to have two youth groups that span the teenage years: a junior and a senior youth group. At what age (or school year) young people should move from one group to another is a matter for debate. In many churches they join the senior youth group in the year they turn 15 or 16. Each church must decide for itself. Segregation by age will create occasional problems, e.g. dividing up friends, but on the whole it is far preferable to having only one group.

Once the dividing age (or school year) is set, avoid making exceptions. It is not uncommon for young people to want to stay in the junior group when they should move up, or to move up to the senior group before their time. Often they want to move up early because the senior activities seem brighter and 'the grass is always greener over the fence'. Girls sometimes want to move up because they are attracted to guys in the older group. Some want to stay in the younger group because they like being the biggest and lose this advantage if they move up; or perhaps they simply don't like change. If they stay in the junior group too long, the danger is that they may eventually lose interest and drop out instead of moving up. On the other hand, if they move up before they are ready, they may become disillusioned with the senior group and drop out with such a negative opinion of the group that they never come back.

Bearing all this in mind, there are occasions when exceptions should be made. But be careful of parents in this regard: it is simply mind boggling how many parents claim that their son or daughter is an exception because he or she is more intelligent, more mature or in some way or other a cut above the rest.

In some situations it may not be possible to divide into two groups—for example, if there is only one youth leader available or there are only a few young people. Here you have to do the best you can, but it is best to aim to divide into two groups as soon as possible.

Give special attention to transitions

When a church youth program involves several groups catering for various age groups, it is important to work hard at helping young people to make the transition from one group to the next. It can be scary to move into a completely new group, especially if you are younger.

During their last year in a group, prepare young people for their coming transition into the next group. Visits from members of the older group explaining how it works and perhaps an invitation to a special activity with the older group will help. When the time comes for youth to join the older group, make sure they are made welcome. Perhaps there could be a special barbecue, dinner or party arranged for their first activity, just to make them feel welcome. One church I know of organises a leader each year to help the young people make the transition from the junior to senior youth group by moving up with them.

It is common for churches to lose many young people in the transition from one group to the next. Sometimes it is because the effort is not made; but in other cases it is because leaders who are more concerned with maintaining the numbers in their own group hinder the transition process. People are held in a group that eventually becomes too young for them, they lose interest and drop out. Then it is usually too late to start talking about the older group.

The goal of youth ministry is not just to entice a group of young people to come to an activity but to prepare them to be mature active members of the church for the rest of their lives. If that is to happen, they must leave the youth group. Many youth leaders resist this and do untold damage. They rationalise this in all sorts of ways but, at the bottom line, having their own following is more important than the spiritual health and development of their group. A good test of the commitment and maturity of youth leaders is seen in how hard they will work to shift young people from their own programs when the time comes.

2. Think clearly

Having considered the broad context of the whole church of which the youth group is a part, youth leaders must think clearly about the individual youth group activities. Many youth leaders rush so quickly into organising their youth group activities that they don't stop to think the activities through. We will be much more effective if we spend more time thinking before we act.

Set specific goals for each activity

In the first chapter, we considered the overall goals of youth ministry and explored how unclear thinking in this area affects the whole process. The same is true of any specific activity. Many of the problems encountered in youth activities can be traced back to faulty goals.

Some youth activities seem to have no goals or only very vague ones. Youth group night has come around again and the youth leader has to find something for the group to do. But merely 'to have an activity for young people' is not good enough. What is the activity supposed to achieve? How will the youth group or the young people in it be different as a result of this activity?

In broad terms, according to the strategy outlined in chapter 2, many activity goals would fit generally into contacting, evangelism and teaching. But the aim usually needs to be more specific than that. Evangelistic activities may aim at more specific goals like:

- helping young people to see that the gospel is true
- helping them to see that the gospel is relevant to life
- teaching basic facts of the gospel
- exposing misconceptions of the gospel
- challenging young people to respond to the gospel.

To say that the goal of an activity is evangelism is usually not specific enough. The same goes for activities designed to teach Christians. What specific things are they to know at the end of the activity? How are their lives to be different? Ideally goals for activities should be *specific, measurable and achievable*.

If the goal cannot be written down in a short statement, it is not specific enough. If your activity is to have a sense of purpose, you must be very clear in your mind as to what you expect the activity to achieve. The goal must be identified *before* you start to plan the activity and must be kept in the forefront of your mind as the activity is planned and presented. That sounds basic, but it is amazing how easy it is to lose sight of the goals in the struggle to pull an activity together.

Some goals don't mix

Probably the most common programming mistake in youth groups is the attempt to do everything in the one activity. The youth leader attempts to run a fun, social event that not only attracts, entertains and evangelises teenagers from the community at large, but also nurtures and teaches the Christians. The program often ends up as an hour or two of fun and games followed by a fifteen minute devotion.

The end result is a general, all-purpose youth activity that does not adequately achieve any of the goals aimed for. The teaching of the Christians is inadequate because the general environment and the presence of the newcomers does not allow them to apply themselves to Bible study and prayer. The evangelism is not as effective as it could be because it is hard to get the young people to settle down and devotions seem like an extra tacked on at the end. In the attempt to both evangelise non-Christians and teach Christians the devotions are likely to fall somewhere in between and do neither well.

It is better to have different activities aiming for different goals, as is suggested in the strategy outlined in chapter 2, than to try and achieve too many goals in the one activity.

This mixing of goals is one reason for behaviour problems in youth groups. Gary used to go to a youth group like that. He went initially because his friends told him about the fun activities. When he got to youth group he really enjoyed the first hour and a half: that was all games. But then the leaders made them all sit in a group while someone talked to them about God. Gary had heard this would happen but he didn't come to hear about God: he came to play games. Now he felt trapped and others in the group felt the same. Consequently Gary and some of the others did not listen and were always getting into trouble for misbehaving during devotions. Gary misbehaved because he was motivated for one part of the program but definitely not motivated for another part.

The level of motivation required is a good guide in deciding what activities can be combined effectively. For example Bible study and prayer can be included in the one activity because they both require similar motivation. Similarly an activity that combines social interaction and contacting is also viable. But an activity that attempts to combine contacting with Bible study is unlikely to succeed because the motivation required to do Bible study far exceeds that required to attend a contacting event. In this case the goals are not compatible.

Evaluate programs effectively

It is important not only to set goals before an activity but also to evaluate the activity afterwards. Evaluation is the step in which you reflect on what went right and what can be improved on next time. Here are three principles of evaluation.

(a) *Always evaluate an activity in terms of its goals.* An activity only succeeds to the degree that it achieves the goals that were set in the planning stage. If the goals were evangelistic, then the activity can only be a success if newcomers were attracted and something of the gospel was clearly presented and understood. If no non-Christians were there but everybody had a good time and the program was of a high standard, the activity failed because it did not achieve its goals. The fact that good things happened does not mean that the activity succeeded. We must be honest enough to recognise when we fail to achieve our goals and we must try to understand what went wrong.

It has already been stated that goals, ideally, should be measurable. If you set specific, measurable goals before the event, afterwards you should be able to see if they have been achieved. One reason why some youth leaders get discouraged and wonder whether they are achieving anything is because they don't set goals and evaluate. Then they don't know if they are actually achieving anything. Don't worry if you don't always achieve all your goals. If you do always achieve all your goals, you are probably setting them too low.

(b) *Solicit feedback from a broad range of people.* When the evaluation of an activity requires soliciting feedback, ensure that you gain information from a representative sample. It is not uncommon for girls to have a different opinion to guys and older teenagers to younger ones. It is possible to be misled by a minority.

(c) *Evaluate an activity in terms of the people it was designed for.* While no-one involved in an activity should be disregarded, special attention must be given to the response of the people for whom the activity was specifically designed.

For example, in a contacting activity it is the response of new contacts that is critical and we should not be too worried if an established Christian group member states that they would have preferred a study on the minor prophets. On the other hand, Bible studies are designed for people who want to know what the Bible teaches. We should not give in to people who claim the studies are too 'religious'. Such people should be catered for in other parts of the program; if they come to Bible studies they must take what they get.

3. Program wisely

To be effective, youth group activities need to be planned not only with a sense of purpose, but in a way that wisely meets the needs of young people. Good youth programs are culturally relevant, help provide young people with a sense of belonging and foster in them a sense of identity. Here are three suggestions for wise programming:

Help young people to identify with the group and the program

(a) *Identification is the name of the game.* During the adolescent years, young people are making their identity choices. They are trying to choose what occupations, values and people they will identify with. This has numerous implications for youth work. It is important that young people have a sense of belonging to the group: that they identify with Christians and Christian values and beliefs. For those who are not yet Christians, the first step in that process is not usually being convinced that Christianity is valid, but an awakening awareness that it would be good to belong to this Christian group. The process begins with a move towards identifying with Christians.

Therefore it is important to encourage this process of identification. The quality of relationships, the image the group projects, the openness to newcomers and the involvement of the group and its members in the broader community all affect the ease with which newcomers identify with the group. But it can also be affected by the types of activities that are organised.

For example, taking the youth group skating or bowling is not likely to be as effective as holding a youth group barbecue or pool party. If young people have a good time skating, they may end up saying to themselves 'that skating rink is a great place'. If they have a good time at an activity that is seen to be produced by the youth group itself, they are more likely to to come away saying 'it's great being at that youth group'. That is, they are more likely to come further in terms of identifying with the group.

This does not mean that youth leaders should never take their groups to entertainment venues like skating rinks or bowling alleys, but we need to recognise that this probably won't achieve as much as activities that the youth group organises itself. We must ask 'How well does this activity help young people identify with our youth group'? In youth work identification is the name of the game. If young people are identifying with the Christian group, we are winning: if they are not identifying, we are losing.

(b) *'I wasn't expecting a Bible study.'* Jane had a great time at the youth group pillow fight. It was her first night at youth group and she couldn't wait to go back the following Friday night. On her way she remembered all the fun she had the week before: sixty screaming teenagers playing all sorts of crazy games. As she walked in the door she was expecting something equally riotous and found fifteen young people praying. Jane had walked in on the level 3 Bible study.

Within the youth group, it is important that activities on different levels have a distinct identity so that people like

Jane don't come to the wrong activity by mistake. There are several ways to do this:

- The use of names. If all level 1 activities are called by one name, level 2 by another name and level 3 by a third name, people can then tell by the names used in the publicity whether the activity is for them.

- Different time slots. If the level 3 Bible study is on Sunday and the level 2 activities are on Friday night, they are not likely to be confused.

- Timing. Even if the group meets only once per week, activities can be identified by the timing. For example, Bible studies could be held every fortnight. This way the people who are not Christians know to come only every second week if they don't want a Bible study.

- Method. The methods used could signify the level. If level 1 was always a sports based drop in centre, level 2 always a coffee shop and level 3 always a Bible study in the youth leader's home, no confusion would arise.

Generate atmosphere

Young people are very much governed by feelings. In their own assessment of activities they place great emphasis on the atmosphere generated. If a program doesn't feel good then it will be judged to be not much good, no matter how well it is organised. It is good to help them grow beyond such emotionally based judgments and decisions; but on the other hand, if we want them to attend and enjoy programs we must aim to produce programs with atmosphere. This is determined not only by what is in the program but also by:

- Timing. A fast moving program generates better atmosphere.

- Size of room. A program for fifteen young people feels better in a room than a large hall.

- Seating. Sometimes it's better to sit on the floor.
- Lighting. Dim lighting might be better in a coffee-shop or youth rally.

Be sensitive to change

Youth programs need both stability and variety. Young people need to be able to go to the youth group with confidence that it will meet the needs they expect it to meet. But within that stability, there should be constant change and freshness. Young people appreciate change and creativity, so keep enthusiasm high with innovations. Whether you are involved in evangelism or teaching programs for Christians, always seek new methods and ideas. Try to take young people by surprise. Make sure your programs are stable but don't allow them to become predictable and don't settle for the status quo.

Not only is change important for variety and freshness; we must keep pace with the constantly changing youth culture. For example, the styles of music we use must be appropriate and up to date. If our programs are to be effective in reaching today's young people, they must change with the times.

▶ ▶

4

first time around

CONTACTING YOUNG PEOPLE
AT THE FIRST LEVEL

▶ ▶

As a rule the starting point for effective youth group evangelism is a well trained, mobilised Christian core group. But if the core group are to evangelise effectively, they must make real contact with the other young people in the community. This chapter explores how to make contact with outsiders.

CONTACT—THE BASE
FOR EVANGELISM

One of the commonly held misconceptions about youth evangelism is that if you organise a really good program and promote it well, lots of young people in the district will come. The better the program and publicity, the more people from outside the church will come and hear the gospel. Now that is partially true: better programs and publicity do tend to attract more people—but usually only within certain limits. Consider the following diagram.

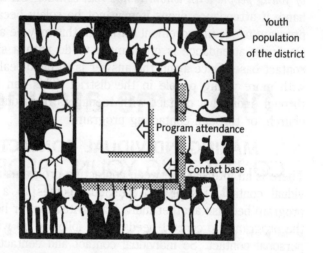

FIGURE 9

Youth population of the district

Program attendance

Contact base

The outermost area represents all the young people in the district. The innermost area represents those who attend any given evangelistic activity. The area in between represents *the contact base.* The contact base comprises all those young people who have a measure of real contact with the youth group through relationships. As a general rule, improving evangelistic programs and publicity will attract more people, but only to the limit of the contact base. Christian teenagers from other churches may also be attracted, resulting in an illusion of contact while in fact teenagers from the community at large have not been contacted. There are exceptions, but most people outside the contact base will not come to evangelistic programs, no matter how good they are, because the youth group and its programs are too far removed from their lives. So while there are exceptions, *on the whole better programs improve the attendance of people with whom you already have contact, but they don't create contact. To grow in its evangelistic outreach, a youth group must broaden its contact base: it must increase the number of young people with whom it has real contact.* On the other hand, if attendance drops it may not be solely because the program needs improvement (although this may be a factor). Declining attendance is often more to do with a shrinking contact base. Once again the answer is to build real contact with more young people in the district. This can be done through individual contact with teenagers from outside the church, or through contacting programs.

MAKING INDIVIDUAL CONTACT

There is an interplay between contacting programs and individual contact. Usually an individual comes to a contact program because another individual invited him or her. After the program the contact needs to be followed up with more personal contact. So individual contact and contacting programs feed off each other, but individual contact is the bottom line. Unless there is real, personal contact with individual young people, how are they going to be invited to a contact program?

Youth leaders need to both make new contacts and strengthen existing contacts. Here are some suggestions that apply not only to youth leaders but also to the young people who are already in the group.

The purpose of contacting

Most people will resist us if they think that we are mainly interested in getting another person along to the youth group. The *goal* of contacting should not be to increase the size of the youth group, but to form friendships through which we can love and serve people whether they come to the youth group or not. In other words, contacting is a bridge building exercise to open the way for ministry. One of the likely *outcomes* of seeking to serve young people in this way is that some of them will come to our programs. But this is only one possible outcome. We must be alert to the many opportunities to serve young people who may never come to our programs.

Where do we contact young people?

Obviously, to contact young people we can't just wait for them to come into our world—we must meet them where they are. We must enter the world of young people and go to the places where they are to be found. Such places vary from district to district but they include cinemas, cafes, pin ball parlours and sporting events. It may pay to join a sports club so that the young people who play that sport can be contacted. Some youth leaders are able to obtain permission to enter high schools and exercise a personal ministry with teenagers. Even with this opportunity it can be hard to break the ice with students. Helping with school sport or some other activity can provide natural ways to get to know students.

Of course building relationships like this is slow work. It takes time to win people's confidence. So take your time and don't push the relationship too quickly. When contacting you will sometimes feel that you are achieving nothing at all and then the opportunities start to come.

Visiting young people at home

One obvious place to contact young people is in their own homes. Most of them live with their parent(s) or some other adult. So when visiting them it is important to not only consider how they might respond to a visit but also how their parents might respond. Sometimes the young people are happy to receive a visit but the parents are not. Some parents would love the youth leader to visit their sons and daughters, who want nothing to do with the youth leader. Each situation must be treated on its own merits.

Usually home visitation is a way of building on to some previous contact. It is a way of following up young people who have already been contacted somewhere else or who may have already begun to come to the youth group. In the early stages of contact you usually need a reason to visit. There are lots of reasons to visit the home if young people have been to the youth group a couple of times. Here are some suggestions.

- Drop in to introduce yourself to their parents. Once young people have been to a youth group a couple of times, their parents are often very keen to meet the organisers and find out more about the group. You never know what opportunities for ministry may arise with the rest of the family. But try to visit when the young people are also at home. That way you can visit them and their parents at the same time and they are less likely to suspect that something may be going on behind their backs.

- Drop in to remind young people of some coming event. Some youth leaders schedule time for visiting people who are marginal to the youth group during the week before particularly attractive youth group events. These young people usually don't mind someone dropping in to let them know that something good is coming up. Often they have not heard—and the visit also helps to build up the relationship.

- Drop in to deliver publicity instead of mailing it.

- Drop in to seek their help or advice on some matter. Many young people have skills that are useful to the youth leader. Some are very good at artwork, music, sport, drama or a host of other things. Instead of seeking help from an adult, you could approach someone from the youth group. Not many adults go out of their way to visit young people and very few adults seek their advice. It usually makes young people feel very special.

Home visitation need not be restricted to visiting young people you already know. Opportunities may arise to visit the homes of those you have never met. A woman once asked me to visit a family in her street where there were a number of teenage boys. She used to pay one of these boys to mow her lawn. I asked the woman what sort of things the boys were interested in and she told me of their interest in cars. It happened that the youth group had planned to have a car rally a couple of months later, so I waited for about six weeks and visited their home one evening. I found the boys working on a car. Having introduced myself, I told them that the woman over the road had asked me to visit them because she thought they might be interested in some of the activities of the youth group. I then invited them to the car rally. They came to the car rally with about three car loads of their friends and they maintained contact with the youth group for some time.

That visit was made possible because I could tell them that someone they knew asked me to visit them. I have had many fruitful opportunities like that. Often it has been a friend, neighbour or relative who has asked me to visit but sometimes it has been a professional person like a social worker or police officer. There are many who recognise the value of youth groups.

Building relationships

The first contact is just the beginning. It is very important to spend time building relationships with new contacts. This can be done by spending time together informally, one to one or in small groups. All sorts of things can be done. Here are some examples:

- going to the beach,
- swimming,
- hiking,
- picnics,
- movies,
- watching TV,
- playing sport,
- watching sport,
- shopping,
- camping,
- sleep overs,
- driving,
- cycling,
- reading,
- homework,
- music
- eating.

The general rule is *do what they like to do, not what you like to do.* The goal is not to talk about the Christian faith but to get to know each other. However, opportunities to talk about Christ may arise.

The ten commandments of individual contacting

1. Pray. Ask the Lord to prepare the way.
2. Serve young people. Find ways to help them (e.g. driving them home).
3. Try to remember names.
4. Be interested in them. Don't talk too much about yourself or your youth group. Ask them plenty of questions and talk about the things that interest them.
5. Encourage young people to introduce you to their friends.
6. Behave as an adult, not an overgrown kid.
7. Be ethical. Don't do things you said you would not do (e.g. proselytise on school grounds).
8. Don't wear out your welcome.
9. Be a missionary. Don't expect to feel totally at home in the world of young people (if you are not their age or come from a different social group).
10. Be patient. Don't be surprised if nothing measurably significant happens for several months.

CONTACTING PROGRAMS—PRINCIPLES

While individual contact with non-Christians is good, involving them in contact programs (level 1) introduces them to the whole youth group. Here are three principles to bear in mind when planning contact programs.

1. Minimise church culture

Make every effort to ensure that every part of the program is as comfortable as possible for new contacts. This means that your program will exclude activities that only Christians do. These are many, but one of the main culprits is community singing.

To most people in western society community singing is so foreign that it is off-putting. Virtually no one outside of religious groups does it. It is very appropriate for Christians at Level 3; it may occasionally be used at Level 2; but it usually makes new contacts feel quite uncomfortable. We should even think carefully about using community singing in evangelistic programs—only use it when it helps newcomers. It seems that Christians often use community singing in evangelism, not because it helps newcomers, but because we like doing it. Are we prepared to miss out on some community singing for the sake of evangelism?

Public prayer can also be off-putting at a contacting event. Opening in prayer at a riotous fun event can seem forced and out of place. Don't misunderstand me. I'm not saying that we should never pray at contacting programs: but we should think about it and only pray publicly if it is appropriate to do so. How would the newcomers feel about the prayer or understand it? Would they enter into the prayer and own it? The point of public prayer is to lead the public in prayer. If those present don't follow, it is questionable whether the prayer ought to be offered publicly. In such circumstances it is better to pray for the event privately.

To contact young people effectively requires a deliberate effort to work cross-culturally. We must fit in with their world—and that means refusing to allow our own cultural baggage to get in the way. When we are planning a contacting program it is helpful to ask questions like:

• Could a secular youth program do this?
• Could a high school run this program?

Eliminate things at this level that only Christians do. This doesn't mean that we do things that are indecent or un-Christian. There are plenty of options available that are decent and wholesome, yet not so foreign to newcomers that they feel out of place.

2. Conserve and follow-up contacts

It is not enough to get contacts to come to one program; we must strive to keep them coming back. It is helpful to get their names and addresses. One way to do this is to have a host or hostess who asks new contacts if they would like to be kept informed of other events the youth group runs, and collects names and addresses. These could be placed on a mailing list and publicity sent on a regular basis. Such people could also be contacted personally by telephone or personal visit. The youth leaders need not be the only people to do this. Youth group members themselves can also do it and it is less likely to look like the youth leader 'doing his job'.

3. Reject the 'big bang theory'

Years ago I had built up a new youth group to about fifteen. I decided to run a big contact event where we would offer free hamburgers to anyone who came as well as providing a good Christian rock band and some fun activities. We promoted the event well, even to the whole high school, and about two hundred students came. The event went off well and a little less than half came back the next week. Each week the attendance decreased so that about six weeks later the attendance was no larger than before the event was run. I was left wondering whether the event had done more harm than good.

The problem was that our contact base simply could not absorb so many new people at once. They came for the hamburgers. But so many new people simply could not begin to belong to a group of fifteen and it is largely the possibility of belonging that keeps people coming. That event attracted lots of young people but it did not really extend our contact base. We fed a lot of people but did not make real contact with any of them.

In hindsight, we would have been more successful if we had invited fifteen new people to a barbecue. A group of fifteen can make real contact with fifteen new people. There is a much greater likelihood that the new people would feel that they could belong and that the group would be much bigger six weeks later. Promotional pushes must keep pace with the contact base. We must ask: *how many new people can the group realistically absorb?* Groups that grow strongly, grow steadily.

CONTACTING PROGRAMS—EXAMPLES

Contacting programs fall into two broad categories that can be called continual programs and one-off programs.

Continual programs

These are programs that run week after week, in the same time slots and with the goal of making contact with non- Christians. Here are two examples.

Drop-in centres

Drop-in centres can take many forms but they are essentially places where young people can drop in, enjoy some friendship and refreshments and take part in some recreational activity. They can cater for different types of people by providing such activities as sport, hobbies, crafts, music, cards or table games.

One youth leader ran a drop-in centre in the form of a group that met weekly to learn and play their guitars. In another case a teacher provided free tuition one afternoon each week after school. Drop-in centres for unemployed young people have provided something useful for them to do or trained them in cooking, sewing or vocational skills. I have seen a church-run drop-in centre that provided pinball machines, computer games and pool tables.

Drop-in centre facilities can be located anywhere that is compatible with the activities. Some churches have built sophisticated gymnasiums. But expensive premises are not a prequisite. One youth pastor made contact with quite a number of high shool students by playing basketball with them after school on the bitumen car park of the church. For many of the examples mentioned above, facilities are already readily available in the form of halls, homes, garages and parks.

Usually drop-in centres are more effective if they adopt a free, informal style. There also needs to be a clear link to the evangelistic activities of the youth group if the contacts are to flow on. Drop-in centres themselves can be used for evangelism if they are run by a team that is skilful in personal evangelism.

Sporting teams

Some Christian groups organise their own sporting teams and fixtures as a means of making contact with young people.

- *Relationships are the key.* Just because a church has a drop-in centre or sporting team, it does not necessarily mean that the young people who attend will automatically move on to evangelistic activities. The effectiveness of both drop-in centres and sporting teams as a means of contact depends largely on the relationships that are developed. Without quality relationships with others in the church, young people rarely move on to become part of the life of the church.

One-off programs

These are contacting activities that are organised by a youth group from time to time as outlined in chapter 2. They should usually occur on a regular basis (e.g. monthly) to maintain continuity of contact. The term 'one-off' is used because each idea would usually only be used once and would be followed by a different idea next time.

In chapter 2 a list of such activities was supplied. This list is developed further below. There are many resource books on youth groups on the market; for a small outlay youth leaders can obtain a wealth of ideas that are useful for contacting programs. The listing below provides some ideas to get you thinking and to give you some concept of the sorts of programs that, if they are organised well, have the potential to contact young people.

In choosing these contact programs, two factors need to be considered:

- *Balance the costs.* Many families cannot afford to pay for expensive youth activities if they occur too often. Expensive activities need to be spaced out between a number of inexpensive activities unless you are working in a particularly affluent community.

- *Balance the work.* Some of these ideas are great but require a huge amount of work to organise. Youth leaders have to determine how much they can realistically do. It is usually unwise to string together activities that require a lot of preparation. It is better to spread them throughout the year.

Most of the ideas listed can also be used for evangelism if some kind of gospel input is included in a natural way.

Listing of one-off contacting programs

This listing contains brief explanations where necessary. After each idea there is a code that gives an indication of the degree of expense that is likely to be involved for young people who come and the amount of work that is likely to be involved in preparation. This is a general guide only. Obviously many inexpensive and simple ideas can be used in expensive and complex ways.

Key:

HC-high cost; MC-moderate cost; LC-low cost.

PW-plenty of work required to organise; MW-moderate work; LW-little work.

Food

- Barbecue [MC/MW]

- Progressive dinner [HC/PW] Youth group members move from home to home, with each course of the meal at a different home.

- Banquet [HC/PW] Meal can be formal or informal or follow various themes (e.g. Chinese, Indian)

- World's largest banana split [MC/PW] Made of guttering and lined with foil. Fill with icecream, banana etc.

- World's largest jelly [MC/MW] Made in a rubbish bin or similar container.

- World's largest spaghetti [MC/MW] Make a large quantity of spaghetti and present initially in one large container.

- Bad taste dinner [HC/PW] Food colouring is used to present the meal in unusual colours. People could dress in bad taste.

- Luau [HC/PW] Hawaiian banquet featuring a whole pig cooked Hawaiian style.

- Hawaiian night [HC/PW] A Hawaiian style party.

Music, dance and drama

- Dance [Costs and work of any dance are variable.]
- Bush dance

- 50's night (or 60's or whatever) Features the music, dances or activities of the era.
- Concert [LC/MW]
- Talent quest [LC/MW]
- Theatre sports [LC/LW] Teams compete with improvised dramas.
- Movie theatre [MC/MW] Set up your own movie theatre for the night with tickets, ushers, popcorn etc.

Out and about

- Scavenger hunt [LC/LW] Teams are sent out to collect a list of items that earn points within a given time.
- Sounds crazy [LC/LW] A scavenger hunt in which teams are sent out with cassette recorders to record a list of sounds.
- Elephant hunt (or any other animal) [HC/PW] Teams follow clues until they find the animal they are hunting.
- Spy v spy [LC/PW] Teams follow clues to locate a disguised mystery person (spy).
- Person find [LC/MW] Teams follow clues to find key people who give them the next set of clues.
- Boat cruise [HC/MW]
- Bus trip [HC/MW]
- An all night series of activities [HC/PW] (e.g. concert, bowling, skating, video, breakfast).

Fun and games

- Rumble [LC/PW] Teams compete in crazy indoor games-chariot races, paper fight etc.
- Crazy auction [LC/PW] Visit parents and collect embarrassing items from the childhood of people in the group. (e.g. dolls, bibs, bottles). Auction them.

- Mini or VW pack [LC/LW] How many can fit in one car?
- Fashion parade [LC/PW] A local store may supply the latest fashions.
- Crazy fashion parade [LC/PW] A comical parade using clothes and swimwear of past generations.

Monster mess

- Mud bowl [LC/MW] Find or create a venue with plenty of mud. Play tug-o-war, long jump, Red Rover etc. -all in the mud.
- Pillow fight [LC/MW] Lots of contests and games can be played with pillows including an all-in pillow fight.
- Custard fight [MC/MW] Use your imagination!
- War games [MC/PW] Set up a mock battle with flour bombs, water bombs etc as ammunition.

Let's party

- Candid camera party [LC/PW] Borrow from parents old photographs, slides, movies and videos of young people during their earlier years. Set up the photographs as a gallery and present a program of slides, movies and videos.
- Fancy dress party [LC/LW] It can be left open or a theme can be set. Examples: early Australian, TV characters; dress in red and white; dress as something starting with 'P' or some other letter of the alphabet.
- Masquerade party [LC/LW]
- Pool party [LC/LW]
- Skating party [MC/MW] Hire out a skating rink and have a party.

Multiple contacting programs

The best approach to contacting may not involve choosing one method or another, but a combination of several contacting programs. For example, one church youth group had a monthly contacting event using the sort of ideas listed above. But it also had a drop-in centre that opened on two days a week after school and a couple of different sporting teams. This required quite a few people, but worked well—each program contacted young people with different interests who were then fed into the evangelistic programs.

Most youth groups must be content to make a start with one type of contacting program. But as personnel become available, the initiation of additional contacting programs should bring into the youth group new young people who were not attracted by the original program.

▶ ▶

5

getting into it

METHODS OF YOUTH EVANGELISM

▶ ▶

There is no more important message than the message of the gospel. Because of what Christ did for us, we can be completely accepted with God here and now. It is extremely important that the young people of each generation hear and understand this gospel and have an opportunity to respond. This chapter is about methods of communicating the gospel to young people. Before looking at them, however, let us consider three principles of youth evangelism that should be integrated with our methods.

THREE PRINCIPLES
OF YOUTH EVANGELISM

1. Evangelism is a long-term concern

Melinda is sitting on her bed looking at her suitcase and thinking about unpacking it. Only an hour before she had arrived home from a Christian weekend camp and she now sits and reflects on the experience. The weekend was great: horse riding, swimming, nice guys and a great atmosphere around the camp fire. How could she ever forget it? The studies also left their mark. There was this guy who talked about God and lots of the things he said seemed to ring true. But it was all very new to Melinda, who had never been to a Christian program before. She is still not sure if she believes there is a God and she wonders if the Bible could really be God's message to human beings.

All the studies at camp seemed to assume these things, but Melinda sits and sighs at the thought of how long it might take to work through those issues for herself. She also ponders on how she reacted to some of the things she heard–like being called a 'sinner'. Melinda knows she isn't perfect, but she isn't the type to do anything criminal or have an affair with a married man. About half way through the last study she realised that 'sin' had something to do with her attitude to God. She sees now that what they meant by 'God' was also quite different to what she had assumed.

At the end of the last study, the leader challenged the group to give their lives to Jesus. That was just this morning and Melinda remembers thinking that these people seem to have something she wants, but she is just not ready yet. Melinda reflects that it would have felt dishonest if she had decided for Christ there and then without working it through. The unpacked suitcase is still sitting on the bed and Melinda sighs: 'I'm interested in this Jesus stuff—but it was all too quick, and now camp is over'.

Most people, like Melinda, take a long time to become Christians. They must work out whether they believe the Bible to be true and what it really teaches and this may involve rethinking such fundamental concepts as 'God' and 'sin'. It may take several months, or even years for someone like Melinda to come to faith in Christ.

That camp was good for Melinda: she began to think carefully about the gospel. It would be ideal if the church that organised the camp saw it as part of a long-term strategy and followed up Melinda in an on-going evangelistic program where she could be helped to work through the questions she is asking. On the other hand it would be a bit sad if that camp was the one and only evangelistic outreach of that church for some time. The likelihood of Melinda becoming a Christian would be greatly reduced.

Doing the groundwork

Unfortunately, much youth evangelism is of a one-off nature like that weekend camp. That's better than nothing; some people do become Christians quickly and sometimes a one-off opportunity is all you can get. After all, the apostle Paul took the one-off opportunity offered at Athens (Acts 17). However it is better to plan to evangelise people over a long period of time. This is what Paul did wherever he could; people like Melinda are more likely to come to Christ when more time is taken.

Doing the groundwork has always been an important part of evangelism. Sometimes in the Bible this is not always obvious. For example, in Matthew 4 when Jesus approached Peter and Andrew and said: 'Come, follow me', it looks a lot like one-off evangelism. But in John 1 we find that on at least one previous occasion Jesus had met them both and spent the whole day with Andrew who became convinced he was the Messiah. So in Matthew 4, when Jesus said: 'Come, follow me', the groundwork was already done.

Sowing and reaping are useful words to describe evangelism. They bring to mind images of farming: clearing the land, ploughing and preparing the soil, sowing the seed, irrigating, fertilising and harvesting. Unfortunately, much modern evangelism seems to assume that harvesting is the only step in the process. Many of our attempts to get people converted quickly betray as little understanding as a farmer who drives his harvester over virgin scrub and wonders why he doesn't get a harvest. If we don't take the time and make the effort to sow plenty of seed, we can't expect much of a harvest.

Sowing the seed involves more than explaining the gospel. Many people will need to weigh up the evidence for the Christian faith and will want answers to questions like:

- How do we know there is a God?
- How do we know Jesus is the Son of God?
- Is the Bible reliable?
- What about other religions?
- Why are there so many Christian denominations?
- Why does God allow suffering . . . or war?
- Does science conflict with the Bible?

But before we begin to help young people to consider the gospel seriously, they may have to question what they already believe. Young people have their own, individual belief and value systems. For many, pleasure is the ultimate end in life: to get as many kicks as you can on the way through. Others give security or status the place of ultimate significance.

Unless young people come to question these values and beliefs, they are unlikely to embrace the gospel or even give it serious consideration. People cannot accept the true and living God unless they reject their false gods. The gospel must be made relevant and challenging to everyday life. These processes of challenging their beliefs, helping them explore their questions and clarifying the gospel all serve to to make evangelism a long-term concern.

2. Strive for quality and relationship

Most young people today have fairly sophisticated tastes and are not moved by sloppy programs. Television and the entertainment industry have raised their expectations so that they demand quality. Therefore if we want to present evangelistic programs that young people find attractive, quality is what we must aim for.

However, quality is not the only consideration. Remember the story of Barbara in chapter 3? She was the youth leader who organised a barbecue followed by some games and a discussion and we noticed that she made a number of delegation mistakes. One of those mistakes was to ask sixteen year old Ryan to sing and he made a mess of it. But Barbara had good reasons to ask Ryan to sing and that is that he was well liked at school. Now that is good thinking on Barbara's part: she recognised the value of involving people who have good relationships with young people and with whom they identify. Her mistake was that she sacrificed quality too much.

Sometimes it may be better to sacrifice a little quality for the sake of relationships. A sixteen year old who is a reasonable singer but is well known and respected may be a better choice than a better singer who is unknown. Similarly an assistant youth leader who is liked and respected may be a better choice for a speaker than someone who is more competent but totally unknown.

There is an old saying 'It's not what you say but who says it that counts'. That's not completely true but it does contain a measure of truth.

Two very practical things are likely to affect the quality of evangelistic programs.

Frequency

Obviously, the greater the frequency with which a program is run, the more difficult it is to maintain quality. For example, it is much easier to run a quality program every month than every week. The benefits of running a program more frequently need to be weighed up against the likely drop in quality.

Workload

Overworking organisers with excessive responsibilities is likely to reduce the quality of the programs they produce. There is a limit to how many things any one person can handle well; it is far better for people to do one or two things well than many things poorly. If possible, spread the load rather than overload the faithful few.

3. Undergird programs with personal contact

Before we consider specific methods of evangelism, let me emphasise that our programs are no substitute for the evangelism that takes place, one to one, in personal relationships. It is most important that youth leaders and Christian young people do the best they can to build friendships through which they seek opportunities to share the gospel.

The New Testament places a high priority on evangelism but when we read it we find surprisingly few programs organised by Christians to which outsiders were invited to hear the gospel. Evangelism was done through natural relationships, or at meetings organised by non-Christians, where Christians were invited to speak.

When Christians spoke in the synagogues, they were speaking in meetings that were organised by people still committed to Jewish beliefs and when Paul spoke at the Areopagus in Athens it was more the equivalent of a guest lecture at a university than an evangelistic rally. In the New Testament, Christians evangelised by taking the gospel to the world at large, not by trying to bring outsiders into a Christian program to hear the gospel message.

This does not mean that evangelistic programs are not valid; if wisely run they can be very helpful, but they need to be undergirded by personal contact if they are to have an impact. The most effective youth evangelism is probably done by Christian young people through friendships at work, school, university or when playing sport.

Some ways to encourage Christian young people to share their faith with their friends include:

• Modelling. Try to find ways for them to watch other Christians care for people and explain the gospel.

• Teach them that they are the most strategic people to reach their friends for Christ. Their caring and friendship can be more effective than an evangelistic program.

• Teach them the gospel so that they can share it.

• Train them to recognise opportunities to share the gospel. Opportunities rarely come with questions like 'How can I become a Christian?' Opportunities usually arise as people discuss the concerns and issues of life. Help young people to think about the opportunities that arise for them and how they might respond.

• Encourage them to keep in close contact with a wide circle of friends.

- Explain that not everyone has the gift of evangelism. All Christian young people can be friendly and caring but they won't all be good at communicating the gospel. They should do the best they can and accept their limitations.

THREE METHODS OF YOUTH EVANGELISM

There are many methods and contexts of youth evangelism. I have chosen to comment on three methods that youth leaders often consider when deciding on a method of evangelism. Camping, while it is a very valuable method, has been omitted from this discussion because it is a big subject and there are numerous books devoted to it (e.g. *The new camping book* by Tom Slater, 1990, Scripture Union). Furthermore, I want to concentrate on methods that can be slotted in to the regular youth program so that evangelism can be sustained on a regular basis e.g. monthly, fortnightly or weekly.

Each method will be dealt with in four sections. First, the method will be *described*. Then there will be comment on the *rationale*: the thinking processes that are brought to bear in using the method. *Points on implementation* will make practical suggestions for making the method work. Obviously, there is a lot more that could be written but the comments highlight some of the more important issues and common mistakes. The final section will be an *evaluation* of each method. This examines some of the strengths and weaknesses of each method and considers the circumstances in which it is most useful. Comments on these methods are of a general nature and it is freely acknowledged that there will be exceptions. It should also be noted that these methods can be used to achieve other goals besides evangelism.

Youth rallies

The youth rally, while probably the method that is least likely to be used by the average youth leader is possibly the first to be thought about because it seems like the most direct method of evangelism.

Description

Rallies are variety programs that are usually staged in concert halls and aim to attract large numbers of young people from church youth groups. The programs usually last a couple of hours or so and involve such things as live music, drama, movies, community singing and an evangelistic address. They are organised like a concert, usually with a speaker at the end of the program (although placement towards the middle is sometimes more effective). Counsellors are often provided and people are encouraged to seek their help if they believe that they have a particular need.

Rationale

Rallies are usually designed to appeal not to non-Christians but rather to Christian young people. The promotion is aimed at church youth groups and the organisers hope that the Christians will bring their friends. That's why many rally programs have community singing: not because everyone relates to it, but because Christians like it. Unless the Christians like the program, they won't come and bring their friends. (I am describing here what usually happens: personally I believe that evangelistic rallies would usually be more effective without community singing.)

Points on implementation

(a) Rallies need to be sharply produced. Good production techniques need to be employed. If stage lights and curtains are going to be used, they need to be used well. Wobbly spotlights and clumsy use of other equipment can be more

than distracting. Similarly, sound production needs to be of high quality. Rallies look ridiculous if not done well. One of the secrets is to have a good production team, good stage manager and thorough forward planning. Ideally, the program should be rehearsed if at all possible. Producing rallies is like playing lawn bowls: it looks easy, but it is very hard to do well.

(b) Rallies need high quality talent. Unless you are in a large city with plenty of Christian talent, it is difficult to find enough talent to run regular rallies. Many regular rallies import talent from other places and consequently have large budgets.

(c) They need a suitable speaker, compere and songleader. Rallies are often built around the personalities of their comperes and songleaders. The choice of speakers is critical. Some seem unable to function in a stage setting and do not cope well with stage lighting. The content of the address must be particularly relevant to young people.

(d) They need good publicity to motivate Christians to come with their friends.

Evaluation

Rallies are very expensive to run and, on the whole, not very useful for evangelising young people who are untouched by the gospel, because usually they won't even come. However, they are useful for evangelising those who are already established in youth groups but have not become committed to Christ. There are plenty of young people like this.

Many youth rallies have been organised by denominational youth departments or para-church groups as a service for local church youth groups. This can have a number of benefits. There are many youth leaders who can run a youth group but have a limited ability in evangelism. By bringing their groups to youth rallies they can provide evangelistic input.

Rallies can also be good morale boosters for small youth groups where young people can easily get the impression that there are not many Christians in the world. When they come to a rally where there are thousands of other Christian young people, it quickly changes the image.

Youth rallies are not as popular as they once were although some still pull them in in big numbers. Much of their role has been taken over by *professional Christian concerts* and some of these Christian artists make evangelism a high priority. Such concerts have all the benefits of rallies outlined above, and in addition some of these artists, because they have already won respect through their music, can attract many young people who have no other contact with Christianity.

Coffee shops

Description

Coffee shops provide a low key, non-threatening environment where young people can relax, enjoy themselves and be exposed to the message of gospel. Usually a venue is arranged with chairs seated around tables, dim lighting and decorations. People are served refreshments from a simple menu while a ministry team sits with them and engages them in conversation.

A program will often be presented and may include music, drama, movies, audio-visuals and perhaps a speaker. However, it is by no means essential to have a program. Coffee shops have been run quite successfully with pre-recorded music playing in the background, simple refreshments and a dedicated team playing cards or table games with the young people. As the team gains their trust, opportunities arise to share the gospel in normal conversation.

There have been instances when the owners of ordinary, commercial cafes and milk bars have welcomed Christians running entertaining, low key, evangelistic programs in their shops. This is a great opportunity if it arises.

Rationale

There are two distinct approaches to programming. The gospel is either *presented from the stage* (through a speaker or some other medium) or it is *shared one-to-one around the table*. If the gospel is declared from the stage, the program must be strong so as to draw the attention of the audience to the stage and set the scene for the speaker. It is very hard for a speaker to communicate effectively if the supporting program has not already captured the audience's attention.

If the gospel is to be shared personally across the table, the program needs to be of a more low key nature to allow people to talk while playing cards, drinking coffee or whatever. The intensive type of program that is needed to prepare for a speaker, if it is imposed on a program that relies on one-to-one communication of the gospel, will only compete with the evangelism. This is because the program will distract the young people from the table conversation. It is very difficult to talk to someone about the gospel (or anything else for that matter) if rock bands are playing loud music all the time.

One way to arrange a sufficiently low key program allowing one-to-one communication of the gospel is to organise attention grabbing brackets interspersed with segments of at least thirty minutes of background music, during which real conversation can take place. Another way is to start with an hour or so of solid program to set an atmosphere and encourage young people to come in, followed by mainly background music for the remainder of the night.

The *advantage* of declaring the gospel from the stage is that you have more control of the content that is communicated and you can ensure that someone does share the gospel.

The biggest *disadvantage* is that many people will walk out on a speaker or film, while they would stay and talk if they were skilfully engaged in conversation. A coffee shop with an evangelistic speaker is little different to a youth rally in a coffee shop setting and, as such, is most effective for evangelising young people who are already established in church youth groups.

The remainder of my comments will be specifically concerned with coffee shops designed to reach unchurched young people who are more likely to respond to one-to-one sharing of the gospel across the table.

Points on implementation

(a) Teach the team. They need both to know the gospel and how to recognise and respond to opportunities to share their faith that arise naturally in conversation. This won't just happen: the team will need to be trained. Two excellent resources designed to develop these skills are *Care to say something* and *Something to say*, both published by Scripture Union.

(b) Actively contact. Unchurched young people are unlikely to come into a coffee shop just because it is there. The coffee shop needs to be linked to some sort of direct contacting where the team meets young people in their own territory.

(c) The location of the coffee shop is important. A highly

visible venue with passing traffic near where young people live or spend time is ideal.

(d) Don't let catering hinder evangelism. Arrange catering personnel so as not to interfere with the evangelism. Sometimes team members are just beginning to explain the gospel when it is their turn in the kitchen. It is not good to arrange a catering shift so that some of the team have to stop talking to contacts to serve coffee. It is better to have the one catering team work through each session.

(e) There is an optimum attendance level. Coffee shops can be so well attended that they become counterproductive. If too many young people come, the whole team is taken up with serving refreshments and no-one is able to share the gospel. Forty to fifty people is probably the most a team of twenty could deal with at any one time and still ensure that evangelism happens. It might look a lot more impressive to have a hundred young people in the coffee shop, but it would be a lot less effective.

(f) Avoid promoting the coffee shop to church youth groups. Coffee shops are sometimes hindered when they are flooded by well-meaning church young people. Unfortunately, such groups tend to create an atmosphere that acts as a deterrent to unchurched young people. You can't keep the coffee shop a secret, but it is unwise to promote it to church youth groups. This is not to suggest that they should not be made welcome; but it is important not to allow them to unwittingly sabotage the evangelism. Where possible it is best to involve them in the evangelism instead.

Evaluation

The effectiveness of most coffee shops depends on the commitment and skill of the team. With a skilful team they are a useful way to reach young people who would not normally go anywhere near a church; and they tend to be most effective with a group that is not too large.

Evangelistic home meetings

Home meetings are used extensively for youth evangelism by church youth groups as well as para-church organisations. One of the easiest and most effective methods available to youth leaders, they can be run on a long-term, ongoing basis (e.g. every Friday evening) or they can be formed for just a few weeks to explain Christianity.

Description

Home meetings are informal gatherings in a home, usually in the living room. They begin with a segment of activities to break the ice. This often consists of games, crowdbreakers or music with the purpose of entertaining and relaxing the young people to create an easy going atmosphere that is conducive to discussion.

The fun and games are followed by the communication of the gospel. Almost any method of communication can be used: talks, discussions, audio-visuals, videos and movies. Regardless of the method used, the key words are 'discussion' and 'interaction': there should always be freedom for young people to discuss the issue at hand and interact with the views of others. It is not only a matter of telling them the Christian view but hearing what they believe and helping them to work the issues through. You will obtain a more enthusiastic response if you cover issues of importance to people unconnected with the church. For example, they are more likely to discuss subjects like 'parents', 'cheating' or 'death' than 'the nature of the Trinity'. It should not be all discussion though: a leader should present a Christian view somewhere in the program.

Numerous resources are available with almost endless ideas for both the games and crowdbreakers component of the program and the discussion or input section.

These meetings often take about an hour and a half followed by supper. They can work with small groups of five or six or with large groups. Some groups of well over a hundred have met long-term in homes. Sometimes such meetings are run successfully in church halls, but people from outside the church are often reluctant to enter church property and the atmosphere of a hall can be a little cold.

Rationale

The strengths of home meetings are neutral ground and the informal atmosphere. Young people from outside the church come much more readily to a private home than to a church building, especially if the meeting is held at the home of a young person they know. An informal atmosphere will encourage them to express their own views openly and interact freely with leaders and other young people. Well run home meetings lack the inhibitions of a formal situation and provide an atmosphere where young people can hear and evaluate the gospel in a non-threatening way and enjoy the fellowship of the group.

Points on implementation

(a) Generate an informal, relaxed atmosphere. The discussion will work much better if the atmosphere is right. This is influenced by all sorts of things like the size of the room and the effectiveness of the preliminary program. If people are laughing and relaxed as a result of games and crowdbreakers which went well, they are much more likely to participate in discussion.

(b) Encourage interaction and discussion. Gospel input is important but be sure to encourage young people to *express*

their opinions. Use discussions and encourage feedback. By hearing what they are saying you are better able to understand what they believe and to discover what they think you are saying.

(c) Home meetings operate best when there is a strong Christian core. Teach the Christian core to set an example in behaviour and to provide Christian input in discussions. A Christian view may have more impact in a discussion when expressed by a sixteen year old rather than the leader.

(d) Choose the home carefully. The home needs to have a living room or rumpus room of acceptable size; seats are usually not necessary as most young people will sit on the floor. It is a real advantage to hold the meetings in the home of a popular young person.

(e) Don't change homes too often. We must continually think of new people in the group. While it may suit the established members to rotate to different homes, newcomers don't know where everybody lives and tend to lose track of where to go next; thus they are likely to drop out. If possible, stay at the same home for several months and then go to great lengths to ensure everyone knows where to go when you do move.

(f) Explain the requirements to the host family. Prior to the first meeting, explain to the host family the goals of the group and give them some idea of what is likely to happen. You may also need to discuss a number of specific issues including:

- Confidentiality. The family may hear young people say all sorts of things which may be unwise to pass on.
- Noise and distractions. The meeting is a serious time for sharing the gospel and distractions need to be kept to a minimum. Ask the family to try to identify the things

that might cause problems and jointly work out what to do about them. The telephone is a common problem as it is often located in the room where the meeting is to be held; there is nothing worse than someone talking on the phone when you come to a crucial part of your talk. Work out what to do if the phone rings.

- Small children. Some small children of host families love to show off to all the big people at youth group even if the youth leader is in the middle of a serious talk.

- Problems. Ask the host family to freely raise any problems that may occur.

(g) Think about where you stage the meeting. Avoid staging the meeting in a location where latecomers will interfere with what's happening out the front. Set up the room so that everyone can be seen by the person leading the meeting.

Evaluation

Home meetings are a very effective method of evangelism for youth groups. Unchurched young people come relatively readily to this type of meeting because of the non-threatening environment. Another plus is that these meetings are inexpensive and relatively easy to run with the huge range of resources available.

6

going deeper

DEVELOPING SPIRITUAL MATURITY IN YOUNG PEOPLE

► ►

We started this book by exploring the goal of youth ministry and we found that a biblical goal is to lead young people to 'maturity in Christ'.

We then looked at a strategy for leading them to maturity and, in the last two chapters, we considered the first two levels of contacting and evangelising. Now, in this final chapter, we will explore ministry on the third level with Christian young people. How can we help them to grow to maturity in Christ?

We will examine four processes that may be involved in developing spiritual maturity in Christian young people: modelling, pastoring, teaching and serving.

MODELLING

Modelling is the process through which we learn by being exposed to other people's lives. It means learning by example and it happens whether we like it or not. If we work with young people, we *are* models. The question is: *are we good models?*

If it was good enough for the apostle Paul . . .

Paul referred to modelling a number of times in his New Testament letters. In Philippians 3:17 he wrote 'Join with others in following my example, brothers, and take note of those who live according to the pattern we gave you'. Paul urges his readers to follow his example and the example of anyone else who lives like Christ. We are to make a point of modelling our lives on such people. Obviously, we are not to imitate them in every respect, but in the areas of their lives where they are like Christ.

In writing to the Thessalonians, Paul applied this principle to whole churches:

> For we know, brothers loved by God, that he has chosen you, because our gospel came to you not simply with words, but also with power, with the Holy Spirit and with deep conviction. You know how we lived among you for your sake. You became imitators of us and of the Lord; in spite of severe suffering, you welcomed the message with the joy given by the Holy Spirit. And so you became a model to all the believers in Macedonia and Achaia (1 Thessalonians 1:4-7).

Note the three steps that took place:

- Paul points out the exemplary lifestyle that he and Silas lived amongst them—'You know how we lived amongst you'.

- The Thessalonian Christians chose to imitate Paul and Silas—'You became imitators of us'.
- Because the Thessalonians modelled themselves after Paul, they became a model for other Christians — 'So you became a model to all the believers in Macedonia and Achaia'.

A few verses later Paul outlines some of the qualities that he and Silas displayed as they lived and worked in Thessalonica. We will return to these qualities but as you read this passage, underline the things that Paul and Silas did and did not do in their ministry.

You know, brothers, that our visit to you was not a failure. We had previously suffered and been insulted in Philippi, as you know, but with the help of our God we dared to tell you his gospel in spite of strong opposition. For the appeal we make does not spring from error or impure motives, nor are we trying to trick you. On the contrary, we speak as men approved by God to be entrusted with the gospel. We are not trying to please men but God, who tests our hearts. You know we never used flattery, nor did we put on a mask to cover up greed—God is our witness. We were not looking for praise from men, not from you or anyone else.

As apostles of Christ we could have been a burden to you, but we were gentle among you, like a mother caring for her little children. We loved you so much that we were delighted to share with you not only the gospel of God but our lives as well, because you had become so dear to us. Surely you remember, brothers, our toil and hardship; we worked night and day in order not to be a burden to anyone while we preached the gospel of God to you.

You are witnesses, and so is God, of how holy, righteous and blameless we were among you who believed. For you

know that we dealt with each of you as a father deals with
his own children, encouraging, comforting and urging you
to live lives worthy of God, who calls you into his kingdom
and glory (1 Thessalonians 2:1–12).

These passages do not merely teach that Paul's words
were backed up by his life: they teach that people learnt
from Paul's life as well as his words. Paul's Christian values
and attitudes rubbed off onto those who knew him.
Modelling is a very powerful process in ministry and it is
particularly powerful with teenagers because of the developmental stage they are at. In their search for identity, teenagers are looking for models to conform to. They must
conform: they can't help but do so. The choice is not
whether they will conform, but to what they will conform. It
is not enough merely to preach sermons which exhort them
'Do not conform to this world'; the church must produce
alternative Christian models for them. If we are to encourage Christian maturity in young people, we must provide
models of spiritual maturity.

The church can provide Christian models on three levels:

(a) Christian peers

A large segment of chapter 2 explored the benefits of
Christian peer pressure.

(b) Christian adults

The adult members of a church, especially the parents,
can have an immense impact on young people. As young
people grow up they will tend to understand Christianity in
terms of what they see in adults they identify as Christians.
This will affect not only whether or not they want to be
Christians, but also their very understanding of what it is to
be a Christian.

Therefore the problems of young people are often reflections of the problems of parents or other adults. We cannot understand the problems of a youth group in isolation from the rest of the church. If the adults in a church are immature, shallow Christians they are likely to have an influence on the next generation. Sometimes young people see through such adults, rebel and leave the church. At other times they don't see through them and grow up exactly the same.

It can be very difficult to teach commitment, service and authentic Christian living to young people when their parents have a materialistic, self-centred lifestyle and yet are active in church. One way or another, these parents give their children the message that *their* lifestyle is Christian and foster the misconception that you can be a Christian without being a disciple.

However, none of this means that every young person who rebels does so because of spiritually immature parents or adult models. Young people have wills of their own and some will rebel against excellent models. (Judas could not have had a better model than Jesus.) Nevertheless, that qualification aside, modelling remains a very powerful factor in the development of spiritual maturity.

So if we are to develop spiritual maturity in young people, our first priority should not be to employ a youth worker or to form a youth committee, but to attend to our own spiritual maturity and to the maturity of the whole fellowship. There will always be exceptions, but on the whole, the spiritual maturity of young people will reflect the available models.

(c) Leadership

Here we will consider the youth leaders and other Christian leadership with exposure to young people. First we must realise that leadership is not conferred by office but is recognised as it is practised.

After finishing speaking at a seminar for youth leaders, I was approached by a young man who asked: 'How do you make the young people follow you?' He went on to explain that he had been appointed to the position of youth leader in his church but none of the young people would follow him. Instead, they eagerly followed another person who was a good influence on them.

His problem was that he believed the church leadership held him accountable for a youth group over which he had little influence. You can't simply appoint someone as youth leader and expect results. A youth leader requires two basic qualifications:

- The ability to lead young people; and
- A life that is a good model of Christian living.

Someone who is lacking in leadership cannot lead the youth group, and an announcement to the church that they have been appointed youth leader will not, of itself, create the ability to lead. On the other hand, if people who are good leaders but poor models are appointed to leadership, they are likely to lead young people the wrong way. The greater the leadership skill, the greater the potential to lead young people with either good or bad results.

Characteristics of a good model

A good model, in the case of a youth leader, displays the following two things.

- A good example of Christian character and
- A good, open relationship with young people.

Good, Christian character alone is not sufficient because it is through relationships that character is revealed and experienced. Christian character that does not enter into relationships is like a light hidden under a bowl. Let's consider again 1 Thessalonians 2:1–12.

What character traits of Paul and Silas are mentioned in that passage? We find reference to courage, honesty, humility, holiness, righteousness, blamelessness, love and hard work. Paul and Silas display openness, gentleness and love and we find that they are genuine: motivated not by selfishness, but by the desire to please God.

What actions were characteristic of Paul and Silas in their relationships? They are described as sharing, caring, encouraging, comforting and urging people to live lives worthy of God.

Neither of these lists is comprehensive, but they do give us an idea of the sort of character youth leaders should strive to develop and the relationships we should try to build with young people. While much could be written about all of the qualities listed above, I want to comment on only one of them — *openness*. It is openness that exposes the model's inner motivation and qualities to young people. Youth leaders are sometimes afraid of this but it can have a very helpful influence. When we are open about our problems it helps young people to work through their own problems. When we are open about our own struggles and failures, young people are able to learn from us how to handle failure and negative emotions (and sometimes how not to). Seeing some of the youth leaders' failures can also help young people to see that you don't have to be perfect for God to use you.

Of course, wisdom must be our guide in all this. There are some things that should not be shared yet other things that can. This is not a plea for recklessness: we should use discretion within a general lifestyle of openness.

We model the words that describe God!

Modelling not only influences behaviour and values; it profoundly shapes the way young people understand God.

Karen seeks counsel from her youth leader because she is aware of her failings and she doubts whether God really accepts her. The youth leader shows her various verses from the Bible that explain God's forgiveness, and even though she seems to understand and accept the Bible, her doubts remain. Many factors could lie behind this but perhaps it has something to do with the way 'forgiveness' is understood in her family. Her mother has always said that she 'forgives' her father, but everybody knows that she holds a grudge against him as she does with most people. The word 'forgiveness' is still used even when when there is no attempt at forgiveness. Maybe Karen thinks that God 'forgives' like mother.

Brian shudders when the Bible class teacher tells him that God is his Heavenly Father because almost all his memories of his own father are negative and unpleasant. The concept of fatherhood is distorted for Brian to such an extent that it means almost the opposite of what the Bible intends.

The problem is that the words we use to describe God refer to qualities that we model in our lives. These are words like father, authority, love, ruler, gracious, merciful and good. We also talk about God's forgiveness and acceptance. When we use these terms to describe God, people will tend to understand them in the way they see them modelled in the lives of others. Thus the way we live drastically affects the way people understand God. How important it is to 'live holy and godly lives'.

PASTORING

By pastoring we mean personally caring for young people.

Make sure it happens

It is very important to ensure that every young person in the youth group has someone assigned to care for him or her.

If this is not planned it is very likely that some will miss out. Even in a group of fifteen with three leaders, the three leaders will probably tend to concentrate on ten or twelve of the young people at the expense of the rest. The ones who are most likely to miss out are the ordinary young people who neither stand out nor create problems.

Unless the youth group is very small, no one leader can effectively care for every young person. It is only possible to form that sort of relationship with a limited number of people. To pastorally care for everyone effectively requires a team. The following diagram illustrates how pastoral care can be structured.

FIGURE 10

The youth group is divided into a number of smaller groups of three to five young people each. An assistant leader is appointed to each of these groups and is responsible to spend time with all of the young people in their group in order to build relationships and care for each one personally. The assistant leaders should be in regular contact with all the young people in their groups and should do things with them apart from normal youth group activities. They should be aware if anyone in their own group is absent from youth group or church, and should take the initiative in encouraging their young people in the Christian life and helping them with problems.

These groups may or may not meet together formally. They could be used as cell groups or discussion groups within the larger youth group, or alternatively you might decide not to let the young people know they have been divided up. It does not matter whether or not the groups are used for any other purpose. Some of the personal ministry skills and ideas described in chapter 4 when we dealt with contacting are also helpful here for building relationships with Christian young people.

When dividing into these pastoral groups, it is best to take existing friendship groups into account. Dividing the group up alphabetically or geographically usually does not work.

The youth leader's main role in pastoral care is to support the assistant leaders and equip them to care for their pastoral care groups. Using this system, youth leaders spend most of their time working with assistant leaders and with the young people who have problems that the assistant leaders are not confident to handle.

Six guidelines for pastoral care

(a) Ensure that assistant leaders are trained at a separate time. Many assistant leaders are not capable of pastoral care for young people unless they are trained. This needs to be done at a separate time to youth group meetings so that assistant leaders can talk about specific problems.

(Developing a leadership team is a key component of effective youth ministry that is too often neglected. There is very little that any of us can do all by ourselves and we multiply our effectiveness when we train others. Jesus loved the masses; but he spent most of his time training a few disciples who would, in turn, evangelise and nurture the masses.)

(b) Monitor assistant leaders carefully. The youth leader needs to be in regular contact with the assistant leaders to provide them with counsel and support.

(c) Emphasise the assistant leader's role as a model.

(d) Build a sense of security and belonging. A major aim of small group interaction is that young people will gain a sense of belonging and mutual caring within secure relationships. In their relationships with their assistant leaders they may also gain a sense of having a big brother or sister.

The small group is also the first place for discipline. The assistant leader should be able to recognise problems early and nip them in the bud so that only serious discipline problems need to be dealt with by the youth leader.

(e) Cooperate in pastoral care with other church adults and groups. The youth group may not be the only people who have a pastoral interest in particular young people. The minister, elder or some other person may take an interest in his or her whole church family. Communicate with each other and try to work together.

(f) Build good relationships with parents and cooperate

with them in nurturing the faith of their children.

The role of counselling in pastoral care

No attempt will be made here to comment on counselling skills; instead here are some remarks about the place of counselling in youth groups.

There are some youth groups which have no teaching and few service opportunities but which allow young people to come along and have fun, with one or two adult counsellors providing the Christian ministry component. The idea is that when the young people have problems they will seek help from a counsellor.

Now that is much better than nothing, but all it amounts to is waiting for problems to occur and then trying to patch them up. It is much better to aim to build maturity through such processes as modelling and teaching so that those problems are less likely to occur. Counselling will always have a place in youth ministry because problems will occur, but it should not usually be the first line of attack. While it is good to counsel a single girl about her pregnancy, it would have been far better if she had been taught about sexual morality.

Of course many young people have suffered a lot of damage before we contact them and a great deal of remedial counselling needs to be done, but the general principle just described still holds good.

What *is* needed is a deliberate strategy to counsel young people for specific roles and events in life. Pre-marriage counselling is the most obvious example. This may not fall to the youth leader, but somebody in a position of spiritual leadership ought to do it. Other times when preparatory counselling may be helpful are when young people are leaving home, taking up leadership positions or entering tertiary study.

TEACHING

Clearly the teaching of the scriptures and Christian truth plays a critical role in developing spiritual maturity.

Some general principles

(a) Be creative. Today's young people are products of modern education and are heavily influenced by the electronic and print media. They are used to creative communication. So if you don't know about creative Bible teaching, find out!

(b) Have a clear objective. To teach effectively, you need to be able to clearly identify how you expect the young people to be different as a result of each learning experience.

(c) Concentrate on real problems, not just symptoms. 'For ten weeks now I have been teaching them about baptism and they are still not baptised'. This remark was made by a Bible class teacher about his class of sixteen year olds. The conversation indicated that he was going to persist along the same line.

Now I suspect that the reason they were not baptised is not because they did not know what the Bible has to say about baptism, but because something was blocking their commitment. What this teacher saw as the problem was most likely merely a symptom of a deeper problem. We need to look beyond the behaviour that concerns us and address the deeper issues. When those issues are resolved the symptoms usually disappear.

So when you see some behaviour in your youth group that you would like to address in the teaching program, ask yourself: 'Why are they behaving this way? Why don't they go to church? Why do they listen to that kind of music? Why do they go to that disco?' When you take the trouble to ask 'why' you may find your teaching program addressing a different agenda.

(d) Help them to understand how they are manipulated by society. Television, films, literature and advertising all present messages. Sometimes the messages are good but at other times they subtly tell us to be materialistic, self-centred or immoral, or to seek pleasure as the main purpose in life.

I am concerned about what young people watch and read. I am more concerned, however, about Christian young people who watch and read without stopping to think about what is being said. I remember one young girl who saw a particular film six times. She failed to recognise in that film the message that life has no purpose or meaning apart from the pursuit of pleasure. It is very important that we teach young people to evaluate what they hear, see and read so that they can identify what is right and wrong instead of uncritically accepting it.

(e) Emphasise practical application rather than mere knowledge. The more Bible knowledge a person has, the better, but the real test is whether they apply the Bible to their own circumstances. So take time in teaching to consider how the Bible can be applied specifically to life. For example, the Bible teaches 'love one another', but we need to go further than that. Work through with the young people what it means to love specific people in their lives. What does it mean to love the teacher who loads you down with homework? What does it mean to love the person who is always picking on you? Pin it down to actions and help them to set specific goals regarding actions and attitudes that require change.

(f) Balance your material. In the last couple of decades the

study material produced for young people has seen a swing away from the basic facts of the gospel and Christian doctrine to the felt needs of young people. In other words, studies are far more likely to focus on drugs, sex, rock and roll, friendship and witnessing than justification, the work of Christ and the message of Paul's letter to the Romans.

Some would argue that it is important to address the felt needs of young people, while others would say that young people will not understand Christian experience until they have understood the objective facts of the gospel. I believe that we need to do both. However in doing so, we ought to always relate one to the other: doctrine must be applied to life and life issues need to be explored in the light of scripture.

What should we teach Christian young people?

Unfortunately, many youth leaders do not stop and identify the material that they want their youth groups to learn. Rather, they decide content on a week to week basis and often choose it to address a problem that has become evident in the youth group. Once again this practice amounts to waiting for problems to occur and patching them up. While current problems will need to be addressed from time to time, it is far better to identify, and then teach, the material that will help young people to grow towards maturity, so that they will be more equipped to face life's problems.

Obviously, the content you need to cover will vary from place to place but there is still a body of material that needs to be considered. The content that I believe should be taught to Christian young people divides up under seven subject headings as follows:

(a) Discovering the Christian gospel
- The Bible: what it is and how to use it.
- Evidence for the truth of Christianity.

- Dealing with doubt.
- Examining other religions and beliefs that challenge Christianity.

(b) The heart of the Christian gospel

- Basic Christian doctrine. In some contexts young people are taught plenty of doctrine outside the youth group and this needs to be taken into account, but there needs to be emphasis on:
- The person and work of the Father, Son and Holy Spirit,
- The gospel,
- Christian identity and self-image.

(c) Christians belong together

- Church fellowship, body life and spiritual gifts.
- Responding to the different views and practices of others in the fellowship.
- Pastoral care for others.
- Being an example.
- Communion and baptism.
- Understanding your own denomination.

(d) What to do with my life

- Issues related to guidance, decision making, careers and study.
- Preparing young people for the work force (e. g. use of money, business ethics).
- Responses to unemployment.
- Considering full-time Christian ministry.

(e) Friendship, love and sex

- Love.
- Sex education.

- Dating and courtship.
- Marriage.

(f) The shape of my life

- Regular Bible reading and prayer.
- Ethics.
- Legalism, license or Christian freedom.
- Relationships to family.
- Relationships to friends.
- Consistent Christian living.
- Models for Christian living.

(g) Eyes wide open to the world

- Christian witness.
- Evangelism.
- Missionary concerns.
- Concern for local and international needs in the areas of health, welfare and justice.

Always teach for commitment

Whether we are teaching for a greater commitment to a Christian sexual ideal or to a Christian basis of authority or to service within the church, we must never settle for merely imparting information. If we want young people to grow, our teaching must challenge them to respond with a greater level of commitment. That response will of course take a variety of forms, but generally involves some sort of concrete action. For example, if we teach them about the needs of the poor at home or abroad, we will challenge them to do something specific (and realistic) about it — pray, get informed, support relevant organisations, write to the government to urge an increase in overseas aid.

SERVING

The involvement of young people in Christian service is often seen as an outcome of maturity but in fact it often facilitates maturity. Consider Colleen's story.

> Throughout my life I have often been involved with handicapped kids, so it has never seemed much of a hassle for me to do things with them. But it wasn't until one camping experience that I really learnt the value of time spent with these children.
>
> Unlike your average camp where you get a break from your kids, it was my responsibility to be with the kids and give them the care and attention they needed. I had to be with them 24 hours a day. I thought this would be an easy task but God knew that I had a few things to learn.
>
> Thinking I could relax was a big mistake. One of my girls was profoundly deaf, so I had to spend all my time being her ears and helping her understand what was happening. This proved to be very time consuming and tiring. My patience was also tested during this camp. Having to sit at every meal trying to make a stubborn young boy eat was a sure way to learn how to be patient and loving at the same time.
>
> God was starting to reveal areas of my life that I was taking for granted. My life was full of happiness and independence, while these special kids couldn't ever expect such things. They relied on us to help with their showers, meals, getting dressed and even—in the smallest ways—understanding God's love for them. Some of them will always have to depend on others to make decisions for them and so will never lead completely normal lives. I learnt to be very grateful that I can do things for myself.

Through this experience, God taught me to have more of a love for and willingness to serve *all* of his creation and not just the parts which are easy to serve.

Looking back on my teenage years, it is very clear that the most formative experience for me as a Christian was not anybody's teaching but an experience of service.

When I was sixteen a man from my church approached me one day and said something like this: 'Ross, there are hundreds of young guys and girls who go to the local dance every Friday night and they don't know Jesus. I'll pick you up at 7:30 pm and we will go and tell them'. Week after week we went to dances, cafes and anywhere else we could find young people. I would give out tracts and look for opportunities to explain the gospel. We finished up running a coffee shop and at one stage we even had a coffee shop going in one of the local cafes.

I can identify three things that this experience taught me.

1. It taught me to think my Christian faith through

I thought I knew the gospel until I tried to explain it in an unsympathetic environment. People hit me with the hard questions and I discovered that what I thought I had learnt in church fell far short of what is credible in the market place. The experience made me go back to my Bible and think it all through again.

2. It taught me to pray

I was driven to pray—because you learn to pray in threatening situations.

3. It challenged my understanding

It didn't take long for me to realise that the traditional methods of evangelism that I was brought up with did not have a hope of reaching those people for Christ. So began my exploration of ways to evangelise young people. It was to be another ten years or so before I arrived at a settled approach but the journey began when I was taken to a dance to give out tracts and made a clumsy attempt at personal evangelism. That experience totally changed the direction of my life.

Service requires young people to do things that they have never done before. I remember one young man telling me at the end of a youth outreach: 'I have never explained the gospel to anyone before this week. I was not sure that I could, but now I have done it and I know that I can go home and keep doing it'. He did.

Young people should be encouraged to serve, not just because of what they can do for others but *because of what service can do for them.*

Ingredients of a good service experience

What are the important elements to build in to a service experience? What sort of experience contributes most to growth? In *Youth ministry: its renewal in the local church* (Zondervan Publishing House, Grand Rapids, revised ed., 1985) Lawrence Richards suggests three ingredients.

(a) Personal involvement. It is too easy merely to give time or money. Young people will grow more in experiences where they have to give of themselves in personal involvement with others.

(b) Cost. Growth occurs when we make sacrifices.

(c) Understanding. Service that requires young people to understand others and to communicate with them directly is more conducive to growth than impersonal projects like food collections.

When you organise a service project for your youth group, build in these ingredients. Avoid projects where young people remain comfortable and distant from the needy. A fund raising event is better than nothing, but it is far better for the young people to serve the needy face to face. Organise the youth group into small work-parties to go to the homes of widows or elderly people and serve them—cleaning, painting, gardening, removing rubbish. Organise young people to take handicapped people out for the day. Whatever the project, make sure that the young people, as well as attending to physical needs, spend time with the needy face to face, showing love and concern for them as whole persons. In this way, not only will the young people come away from the experience with a better understanding of the people they have served; the needy also feel valued, having experienced real relationships and expressions of love. This sort of service is far more likely to gain a positive response than that which may be perceived as mere charity.

There is a much greater cost to this kind of service but to learn to make sacrifices for others is perhaps the most important lesson for a young Christian. To Richards' ingredients I will add three guidelines of my own.

(a) Don't make service too easy or too tough. Young people need a controlled ministry experience, which offers a challenge or is even a little threatening; don't, however, give them something that is beyond them.

(b) Provide plenty of support. Be available to help, counsel and encourage.

(c) Young people must be allowed to fail. They need to be able to try out their talents and experiment with different roles and responsibilities to see where their gifts lie. All this implies the risk of failure. If young people are to get the most out of service, they need to know that they can fail yet

still be supported and accepted. Failure can be part of the growing process; when we don't allow for the possibility of failure, we limit the probability of growth.

CONCLUSION

Sound youth ministry starts with leaders who are good models, with a heart for God and for young people. The next step is to clearly think through the goals we are trying to achieve and devise ways to contact young people, evangelise them and lead them to maturity in Christ. May God raise up many more of his people who are willing and able to do so.

▶ ▶

postscript 1

BUILDING A YOUTH GROUP FROM SCRATCH

▶ ▶

Building a youth group from scratch is a daunting task but it can be done. To sustain a youth group you basically need three groups of people:

1. An adult support group for prayer, financial and moral support. They will provide lots of practical help and can be a source of great wisdom. Without them, you can end up isolated and under great stress. If you are working from a church base, the church fellowship should meet this need.

2. A Christian core. Without a Christian core young people who are not Christians will lack peer models of Christianity and will have a limited relationship link with the church.

3. Contacts outside the church.

To develop a strong ministry, you need to build in each of these areas. The steps you will need to take, however, will depend on your particular group. Many church youth groups have the Christian young people to make up a Christian core (level 3) but they need to attract outsiders. If you consistently employ the three circle strategy outlined in this book, you should build a contact group (level 1) onto the core (level 3). After you have won the confidence of the contact group, you should be able to begin an evangelistic program (level 2). The three circle strategy is quite workable whether the core group is large or small. With a large group there is always the dynamic that 'a crowd attracts a crowd', but a small group also has strengths. It is more intimate, it is easier to manage and it can be more mobile and flexible. So three or four Christian young people can be a viable start for a youth group outreach.

I have been involved in a number of groups that began with a handful of Christians and eventually grew quite large. There is an advantage in starting small in that you can build a quality foundation much more easily. In any event, it is probably a wise move to begin by strengthening the core group and preparing them for outreach. Three months of group building and training in evangelism would not go astray before the first contacting activity is held.

Some people want to build a youth group where they can contact non-Christians, but they have no Christian young people to form a core. Here you have to work from the other direction: the leaders must evangelise and build a Christian core from the converts. One or two young people plus the leader can form a Christian core.

When building the core group, it is best to aim for quality and not quantity, so that it becomes a group where young people care and pray for each other and take the Bible seriously. Avoid the temptation to build attendance at the core group by dropping the standard. It could take several years to build a core group in this way but it is worth persevering.

Building a youth group from scratch is slow, hard work and often very little seems to happen for a long time. It is sacrificial work: usually the group won't grow unless someone is prepared to get involved in other people's lives. Yet the long-term results are usually more than worth it for those prepared to take the time and make the effort.

▶ ▶

postscript 2

SUCCESSFUL USE OF THE STRATEGY: TWO ACCOUNTS

▶ ▶

THE THREE CIRCLE STRATEGY APPLIED IN A LOCAL CHURCH

We were volunteer leaders in a youth group for the first time. The minister invited fifty teenagers to a barbecue and pool night for us all to meet each other. Once there, we were to take over. We tried to run pool games but no-one wanted to obey the rules; cheating was rife and game equipment was broken. Teenagers were sitting up the street and some were smoking. After a rowdy barbecue, it was time for devotions; we tried some choruses but couldn't get much cooperation. Young people were coming and going while some were in a corner singing their own songs. The short devotion fell on deaf ears. After supper, they all went home . . . we think!

Afterwards, we commented 'We were just police all night long'. After weeks of similar policing social events we looked for help. The three circle strategy was explained to us and we decided to commit ourselves to it 100 per cent.

To build a core group we stopped all social events, only running a weekly Bible study. We soon found our keen Christians. Eight teenagers were then nurtured. Once they were strong and keen to see others coming along, we introduced level 2, once a month. This encouraged the core group, by adding new young people and involving them in outreach. Three months later, we introduced the social outings. Now the basic element was 'Christian'. The three circle strategy was fully operational and effective. The youth group we were policing 12 months earlier was now growing in Christ; it was community minded and had tripled its size (i.e. after dropping initially from 50 to 8 it went way past the original attendance to stabilise at 150).

Three years later, they were ready to go on a mission to an outback township and make an impact of eternal value. Some of the original core group are now leaders of their own core groups and mission outreaches.

Using the three circle strategy helped change young people's lives so they could be effective for Christ.

Ivan and Karen Memmott.

(Ivan and Karen are from a church in southern Queensland and have two small children. Ivan is a panel-beater.)

THE THREE CIRCLE STRATEGY APPLIED IN A SCHOOL SETTING

I have adapted the three circle strategy as outlined in this book within a school setting and have experienced a high degree of success.

Two years ago, the strategy was implemented within a group which had dwindled to 5 students due to older pupils leaving for jobs and further study. There was a strong core of Christian teachers involved in Inter-School Christian Fellowship.

The group met weekly at lunch time, observing a cycle of two core events, followed by a contact event, then an evangelistic meeting. Our meetings were supplemented with daily morning prayer meetings and contact events out of school time once or twice a term. This pattern has been extremely successful.

Through the application of this strategy, involving a heavy emphasis on camping, the core group has grown to forty and we are now attempting to address issues such as the effective care of a larger core group.

An indication of the success of this strategy is that attendance at evangelistic and contact events has always been roughly double the attendance at core meetings. This has happened at every stage in the group's growth. We are finding our contact and evangelistic events are now attracting 70 to 80 students.

I strongly recommend the use of this strategy, not just to increase the size of a group, but as a means of drawing young people to maturity, giving them a vision for winning their friends and a means by which it can be achieved.

Its success, however, is dependent on the leaders' willingness to model this process.

Mark Laraghy.
(Mark is a teacher at Cleveland High School, Queensland, where he also leads the Inter-School Christian Fellowship.)